Twayne's English Authors Series

EDITOR OF THIS VOLUME

Herbert Sussman

Northeastern University

Charles Kingsley

TEAS 273

Charles Kingsley

CHARLES KINGSLEY

By Larry K. Uffelman
Mansfield State College

TWAYNE PUBLISHERS
A DIVISION OF G. K. HALL & CO., BOSTON

Copyright © 1979 by G. K. Hall & Co.

Published in 1979 by Twayne Publishers,
A Division of G. K. Hall & Co.
All Rights Reserved

Printed on permanent/durable acid-free paper and bound
in the United States of America

First Printing

Library of Congress Cataloging in Publication Data

Uffelman, Larry K
Charles Kingsley.

(Twayne's English authors series ; TEAS 273)
Bibliography: p. 150–57
Includes index.
1. Kingsley, Charles, 1819–1875 — Criticism and interpretation.
PR4844.U3   823'.8   79-13295
ISBN 0-8057-6752-5

For Donna, Erich, and Jonathan

Contents

About the Author

Larry K. Uffelman studied at Illinois Wesleyan University, the University of Illinois, and at Kansas State University. At present he is a Professor of English at Mansfield State College in Mansfield, Pennsylvania.

Professor Uffelman has been a staff bibliographer for *Abstracts of English Studies* and for the Research Society for Victorian Periodicals. As the Society's bibliographer, he edits the checklist of periodicals research published annually in the *Victorian Periodicals Newsletter*. His previous publications have appeared in the *Bulletin of the Kansas Association of Teachers of English, The Serif, Kansas Quarterly,* and *Victorian Periodicals Newsletter*.

Preface

Charles Kingsley's career was extremely varied, even for that of a
Victorian man of letters. He produced volumes of sermons, novels,
a play, prose idylls, poetry, reviews, and essays on history and
applied science. He encouraged improved sanitation and public
health. Furthermore, he was involved in disputes concerning
theology and social reform, and he was one of the early supporters
of Darwin's views on evolution. Living and writing from the center
of the mid-Victorian age, Kingsley became an eminent Victorian
whose life and works mirror that age.

His life is both important and interesting. It is, in fact, possibly
more interesting than his works, an attitude indicated by the pre-
dominance of biographical over critical studies. For many, Charles
Kingsley is a name encountered in college or graduate school or in
books about the Victorian age, or else it is associated with the Condition of England Question, John Henry Newman's *Apologia pro
Vita Sua,* or with one's childhood memories of *The Water-Babies*
and *Westward Ho!*

My purpose in this book is, first, to introduce Kingsley to those
who know little about him and who wish to know more. For this
audience, my study is a beginning. Second, my study provides a
critical evaluation of Kingsley's literary achievement. For an
audience already familiar with Kingsley and his work, my study is,
therefore, a review and an interpretation. For both audiences, my
study emphasizes the many strengths of Kingsley's art and shows
that in spite of the difficulties his literary work occasionally presents to twentieth-century readers, who have been reared on different conventions, it still rewards serious attention.

My purposes, the format of the Twayne series, and the general
audience's lack of familiarity with Kingsley have dictated the or-
ganization of my study. I have limited this book to a consideration
of Kingsley's literary work. In Chapter 1, I have introduced Kingsley's work chronologically; in the following chapters, however, I
have grouped them thematically. For Kingsley, the question of
artistic development is not as important as the greater coherence

gained by thematic arrangement. Likewise, my discussion of each novel is preceded by a plot summary. These summaries are lengthy, but they are necessary since novels such as *Two Years Ago* are scarcely vibrant memories among modern readers. They are also necessary to convey the "feel" of the novels. Finally, in my discussion of each work, I have noted the relationship of the work to the age, but I have concentrated on it as literature, focusing on plot, character, and setting. I hope my study will serve its audience well by acquainting it with Kingsley's literary work, by providing an evaluation of Kingsley's achievement, and, through the annotated checklist included at the end, by pointing the way to more specialized studies.

LARRY K. UFFELMAN

Mansfield State College
Mansfield, Pennsylvania

Acknowledgments

I wish to thank Mansfield State College for awarding me a sabbatical leave at a critical time and Radley College, Abingdon, Oxon., for providing me a home away from home. I also wish to thank the Cornell University, Pennsylvania State University, Arizona State University, and Knox College libraries for their assistance and cooperation. Others deserving thanks are my department chairman John Saveson; my colleagues Larry T. Biddison and Jay Gertzman, who offered trenchant criticism; and David Wood, who assisted with bibliographical matters. The dusty labor of the Mansfield State College library reference staff, particularly that of Jeanne Fessenden, interlibrary loan librarian, was of incalculable value at every stage of preparation. I am, moreover, indebted to the editors of the Twayne English Authors Series for their patience and to Herbert Sussman, my field editor, whose suggestions improved my book.

I also wish to acknowledge Kingsley scholars, past and present, whose work I have read with interest and admiration. But a special word of thanks must be reserved for my wife and sons, who have lived with and around this book: Donna critiqued my work at various stages of preparation and typed the manuscript; Erich and Jonathan provided comic relief.

Chronology

1819   Charles Kingsley born July 12 to Charles Kingsley, Sr., and Mary Lucas Kingsley.

1831   Witnesses Bristol Riot.

1832   Student of Derwent Coleridge at Helston.

1836   Family moves to London.

1837   Student at King's College, London.

1838   Matriculates at Magdalene College, Cambridge.

1839   July 6, meets Frances (Fanny) Eliza Grenfell.

1842   February, leaves Cambridge to read for Holy Orders; July, becomes curate of Eversley Church, Hampshire.

1844   January, marries Fanny Grenfell; May, becomes rector of Eversley Church; summer, begins correspondence with Frederick Denison Maurice.

1848   Publishes *The Saint's Tragedy;* anonymous publication of "Why Should We Fear the Romish Priests?" *Fraser's Magazine;* appointed Professor of English Literature and Composition, Queen's College, London; observes Chartist demonstration; meets John Malcolm Ludlow; begins association with Christian Socialists; "Workmen of England" anonymously and "The National Gallery" under pseudonym "Parson Lot" in new journal *Politics for the People;* anonymous publication of poems; articles and series of "Letters to the Chartists" under pseudonym "Parson Lot"; *Yeast* anonymously and serially, *Fraser's Magazine.*

1849   *Twenty-Five Village Sermons; Introductory Lectures, delivered at Queen's College, London;* begins reviewing for *Fraser's Magazine.*

1850   Helps found the *Christian Socialist, a Journal of Association;* helps organize Society for the Promotion of Working Men's Associations; a tract, *Cheap Clothes and Nasty; Alton Locke, Tailor and Poet.*

1851   Preaches controversial sermon at St. John the Evangelist, London; *Yeast: A Problem* in volume form; poetry and a series of articles in the *Christian Socialist* under pseudonym

"Parson Lot"; "The Nun's Pool," the *Christian Socialist;* articles and reviews, *Fraser's Magazine.*

1852   *Phaeton; or Loose Thoughts for Loose Thinkers;* begins publishing *Hypatia; or, New Foes with an Old Face, Fraser's Magazine;* the *Christian Socialist* fails.

1853   *Hypatia; or, New Foes with an Old Face* published in two volumes.

1854   *Alexandria and Her Schools; Sermons on National Subjects; Who Causes Pestilence?;* "The Wonders of the Shore," in *North British Review.*

1855   *Westward Ho!* published in three volumes; *Glaucus; or, The Wonders of the Shore; Brave Words for Brave Soldiers and Sailors.*

1856   *The Heroes; or, Greek Fairy Tales for My Children.*

1857   *Two Years Ago.*

1858   *Andromeda and Other Poems.*

1859   Appointed chaplain to Queen Victoria.

1860   Appointed Regius Professor of Modern History, Cambridge.

1861   Appointed tutor to Prince of Wales.

1862   *The Water-Babies: A Fairy Tale for a Land-Baby, Macmillan's Magazine.*

1863   *The Water-Babies* published in volume form.

1864   *The Roman and the Teuton; What, Then, Does Dr. Newman Mean?* leads to dispute with Newman.

1865   *Hereward, the Last of the English, Good Words.*

1866   *Hereward the Wake, "Last of the English,"* in two volumes.

1868   Begins publishing "Madam How and Lady Why," in *Good Words for the Young.*

1869   Appointed Canon of Chester; leaves on trip to the West Indies.

1870   *Madam How and Lady Why; or, First Lessons in Earth Lore for Children* published in volume form; organizes nucleus of the Chester Natural History Society.

1871   *At Last: A Christmas in the West Indies.*

1872   *Town Geology;* President of the Midland Institute, Birmingham.

1873   *Prose Idylls, New and Old;* accepts stall at Westminster Abbey.

1874   *Health and Education;* trip to America.

1875   Dies.

CHAPTER 1

Life and Times

I *Preparation*

AMONG those who became eminent Victorians, Charles Kingsley, clergyman, social reformer, novelist, and poet, became one of the most eminent. His interest and active participation in social and sanitary reform movements, his lifelong celebration of married love and family life, his intense Protestantism and strong anti-Catholic bias, his intense pride in being British, and his passion for the natural sciences mark him in both substance and tone as one of the principal spokesmen of his age.

On June 12, 1819, three weeks after the birth of Victoria, Charles Kingsley was born to the Rev. and Mrs. Charles Kingsley, Sr., "at Holne Vicarage, Devonshire, under the brow of Dartmoor."[1] In 1831, following a series of moves necessitated by his father's profession, the impressionable young Kingsley was attending school in Clifton when the Bristol Riot occurred. He later characterized this event as his "first lesson in what is now called 'social science.'"[2] The twelve-year-old boy observed the fires and the looting; he saw the corpses lying in the street and the mounted soldiers awaiting orders to disperse the mob.[3]

In 1832, Charles was sent to Helston Grammar School, where he was tutored by the Rev. Derwent Coleridge, the second son of the poet, and later by the young naturalist C. A. Johns.[4] In 1836, Mr. Kingsley was appointed to St. Luke's Church, Chelsea, necessitating the family's removal from the West Country, which young Charles loved and in which he had begun botanic and zoological probings which would interest him for the rest of his days.

In the autumn of 1838, Charles matriculated at Magdalene College, Cambridge, where, like many university men of his generation, he suffered a period of religious doubt. During his life,

Kingsley fought recurring battles with depression over what he termed "the riddle of life and this world."[5] In 1839, however, his doubts were particularly severe. To Frances Grenfell, whom he met in Oxfordshire on July 6, 1839, and with whom he immediately fell in love, Charles revealed the extent of his trouble:

Before he left Oxfordshire, he was so far shaken in his religious doubts, that he promised to read his Bible once more — to pray — to open his heart to the Light, if the Light would but come. All, however, was dark for a time; and the conflict between faith and unbelief, between his hopes and fears was so fierce and bitter, that when he returned to Cambridge, he became reckless, and nearly gave up all for lost.[6]

But, having fallen in love with Frances, religious doubt was not Charles's only problem.

Compounding his difficulties was the opposition of the Grenfells to any communication between the two lovers. The Grenfells were a family on the rise; Charles had no prospects. Still, letters were exchanged, and in 1841 Charles thanked Fanny for sending him copies of Carlyle's works and Coleridge's *Aids to Reflection* and testified to the increasing seriousness of his study.[7] Thus with Fanny's guidance and the influence of Coleridge and Carlyle, Charles began to solve his religious problems and became steadily more interested in a clerical career.

Also in 1841, Charles completed his Cambridge examinations, receiving a first in classics and a second in mathematics. In February 1842, he left Cambridge and began to read for Holy Orders. On July 17, at the age of twenty-three, he took his first service as curate at Eversley Church, Eversley, Hampshire, "little thinking that with a short interval it would be his home for thirty-three years."[8]

When Kingsley arrived at Eversley in 1842, he found himself the curate of a derelict rector and a neglected congregation. The patron of the living, Sir John Cope, resided in his house at Bramshill Park. He had been a companion to the Prince Regent and was interested more in foxhounds than in the state of his parish. Ordination as priest in July 1843 brought Kingsley a slight improvement in his fortunes, for his father was then able to arrange a sinecure clerkship at St. Luke's, Chelsea.[9]

The consequent increase in income and the intervention of the Rev. Sidney Godolphin Osborne, Fanny's influential brother-in-law, combined with the promise of a better living at Pimperne, Dorset, caused the Grenfells to accept Charles.[10] On January 10, 1844, Charles and Fanny were married in Bath by the Rev. Sidney Osborne. In April 1844, the Kingsleys were to move to Pimperne; however, in March the rector of Eversley, absconding with parish funds, fled the country in disgrace.[11] Led by the churchwarden, the Eversley parishioners then requested that Charles be appointed to the now vacant living. In May, Charles and Fanny moved into the damp and rotting rectory.[12]

The rectory as well as the parish was sorely in need of labor. Ponds around the house overflowed into the kitchen during heavy rains, dry rot attacked the beams, books and clothes mildewed easily, and prints spoiled on the walls.[13] In the parish, the illiteracy rate was high, religious instruction was nonexistent, communion was served only three times a year, and attendance at Sunday services was low and undependable.

For the new rector, reform began at home: Kingsley drained the ponds and worked steadily at repairing the rectory. In the parish, he established a variety of clubs, an adult evening school, a lending library, a lecture series, and a loan fund.[14] In addition, he began daily visits among his parishioners and experimented in his own garden with scientific agricultural methods.[15]

In 1845, Kingsley accepted an honorary canonry in the Collegiate Church, Middleham, Yorkshire. He kept this stall until 1856, when the deanery was abolished.[16] Also in 1845, Rose, the first of the Kingsley's four children, was born. She was followed by Maurice in 1847, by Mary in 1852, and by Grenville in 1858.[17]

During 1846, Kingsley began to rewrite the life of St. Elizabeth of Hungary, which he had begun in 1842 as a wedding present for his wife. The blank-verse drama *The Saint's Tragedy,* published in 1848 by John Parker with a preface by the controversial theologian Frederick Denison Maurice, was the result of his labor.[18] The play strikes what was to become a familiar chord:

If . . . this book shall cause one Englishman honestly to ask himself, "I, as a Protestant, have been accustomed to assert the purity and dignity of the offices of husband, wife, and parent. Have I ever examined the grounds of my own assertion?" . . .

If, again, it shall deter one young man from the example of those miserable dilettanti, who in books and sermons are whimpering meagre second-hand praises of celibacy . . . .

If, lastly, it shall awaken one pious Protestant to recognise, in some, at least, of the Saints of the Middle Age . . . *Protestants,* not the less deep and true, because utterly unconscious and practical then . . . will my little book indeed have done its work. (XVI, p. 8)[19]

Kingsley's emergence into the literary world in 1848 was also marked by his appointment as Professor of English Literature at Queen's College, London.[20] Furthermore, while *The Saint's Tragedy* was still in proof, Kingsley wrote for *Fraser's Magazine,* also published by Parker, an article entitled "Why Should We Fear the Romish Priests?" This article developed in argumentative prose the theme of his play and marked the beginning of a long association with *Fraser's.*[21]

II *Christian Socialism*

The year 1848 was an important one for Kingsley. It marked his public appearance as both a literary figure and a Protestant apologist, two roles which were for him frequently indistinguishable. More significantly, however, 1848 was a year of revolution abroad and of Chartist demonstration in England.

Chartism, a working-class national movement which took its name from the People's Charter, a document published in 1838, sought equal electoral areas, universal suffrage, payment of members of Parliament, no property qualifications for voting, vote by ballot, and annual Parliaments. Dissatisfaction among the radicals with the Reform Act of 1832 combined with hunger among the working class and the dream of a new social order to produce these six points. But the Chartist movement failed in 1839; it was revived in 1842, when it failed for a second time. The third and last great revival occurred in 1848, when the Chartists again circulated their petition, intending to present it in a mass demonstration to the House of Commons on April 10. Fearing violence, the government massed its forces, and the demonstration was prevented.

Kingsley went to London in early April to observe the Chartist crisis for himself and to do what he could to help avert a riot. On April 10, accompanied by the Christian Socialist John Ludlow, whom he had met through F. D. Maurice, Kingsley witnessed the Chartists' failure. As the day ended, the Chartists were confused and humiliated, not riotous, and Kingsley and Ludlow retired to Bloomsbury to confer with Maurice.[22] On April 11, Kingsley reported to Fanny that he was "helping in a glorious work" and that together with a group of like-minded persons who had gathered round Maurice he had been up until 4:00 A.M. writing placards.[23]

Thus, out of the failure of Chartism grew Kingsley's active participation in the Christian Socialist movement, a participation which remained active until 1852.

Kingsley's first contribution to the movement was a placard addressed "Workmen of England!" and signed "A Working Parson." In it, Kingsley assured the workers that the clergy recognized the wrongs working men were suffering and asserted that although the Charter was not actually bad it was incapable of curing basic ills. Unable to provide true freedom, the Charter actually would produce slavery to "every spouter who flatters . . . self-conceit, and stirs up bitterness and headlong rage . . . . " Kingsley then proclaimed that true freedom cannot exist without virtue, nor "true science without religion," nor "true industry without the fear of God, and love to [one's] fellow citizens." He closed, declaring that freedom will come with wisdom, because when the workmen are wise they *"must* be free, for [they] will be *fit* to be free."[24]

On April 12, Kingsley informed his wife that he and his group together with Parker were planning a periodical to be edited by Maurice and Ludlow, published by Parker, and called *People's Friend*.[25] The title was changed to *Politics for the People,* and the first number appeared on May 6.[26] For this shortlived periodical (it failed in July), Kingsley provided a wide-ranging group of contributions: essays on the British Museum and the National Gallery, poetry, and political-religious propaganda pieces under the pseudonym "Parson Lot."

While he was fully engaged in his parish work at Eversley and with his contributions to *Politics for the People,* Kingsley began work on his first novel, *Yeast,* which he published serially in *Fraser's Magazine.*

Exhausted and ill after the political agitation of 1848 and the strain of completing a novel for John Parker, who worried that it was hurting the circulation of *Fraser's,* Kingsley resigned his Queen's College Professorship, placed his parish duties in the care of his father, and took his family to Ilfracombe for the winter. There he recuperated by walking along the seashore, gathering specimens and shells, and talking with friends.[27]

In March 1849, however, James Anthony Froude brought controversy to Kingsley's West Country retreat. Froude had resigned his Oxford fellowship in February following the burning of his novel *The Nemesis of Faith* during a university lecture, and Kingsley had agreed to take him in. In April, the Kingsleys moved to Lynmouth and Froude went along, causing Kingsley to spend the springtime defending him.[28] By the time summer arrived, Kingsley was returning to his parish duties, and Froude was successfully courting Fanny's sister Charlotte.[29]

Kingsley returned to Eversley by way of London, where he visited with Ludlow, Maurice, and Carlyle, attended Chartist meetings, and continued to brood over his plan for a new novel to be called *The Autobiography of a Cockney Poet.*[30] Back in Eversley by mid-June, Kingsley picked up his full round of parish duties in an unhealthy season. Cholera appeared in England, and a "bad low fever" settled into his own parish. By early August, his health was breaking down again; consequently, he returned to the West Country for a rest. He fished, read Rabelais and Ruskin, and thought.[31]

In September, Kingsley returned to Eversley. With the money earned from reviewing for *Fraser's* and from the publication of a set of *Village Sermons,* he was able to pay a curate. Thus, in October Kingsley toured the cholera district of Bermondsey, where the sight of filth and its unhealthy consequences shocked him profoundly. He immediately decided to help by joining with friends to haul fresh water into the district and by discussing health and sanitation problems with Bishop Wilberforce. In November, Kingsley wrote to Ludlow, urging him to inquire into the possibility of serving nuisance notices under the provisions of the Health of Towns Act, holding a series of public meetings, and forming a Sanitary League.[32]

In December, he told Ludlow that he had been "shamed and sickened" by a *Fraser's* article detailing living conditions among the poor. He added that except for the portion dealing with tailors, the facts were new to him. He then asserted that although he knew little about association, he was sure it was the workers' only hope.[33] On January 8, 1850, the Christian Socialists met and sponsored their first cooperative association with a group of tailors managed by Walter Cooper, who provided Kingsley with first-hand knowledge of the lives of tailors. At work on *Alton Locke,* Kingsley took time to write *Cheap Clothes and Nasty* for a series, "Tracts by Christian Socialists," which was being produced by his friends from the defunct *Politics for the People.*[34]

When he had completed *Alton Locke, Tailor and Poet,* Kingsley offered it to John Parker. Parker, however, rejected the novel on the grounds that he had suffered from having published *Yeast* and *Politics for the People.* In seeking a different publisher, Kingsley obtained the aid of Carlyle, who recommended it to Chapman and Hall. They accepted it.[35]

Early in 1850 Kingsley was upset by the circulation among workmen of Strauss's *Life of Jesus,* newly translated by Mary Ann Evans, who was later famous under the pseudonym George Eliot, and by "the spread of infidel opinions among the working classes."[36] He wrote to Ludlow about starting a new journal along the lines of *Politics for the People.* This new journal would allow a format for denouncing Strauss "as a vile aristocrat, robbing the poor man of his Saviour — of the ground of all democracy, all freedom, all association — of the Charter itself."[37]

On November 1, 1850, the first number of the *Christian Socialist, a Journal of Association, Conducted by Several of the Promoters of the London Working Men's Associations,* edited by John Ludlow, sold for a penny. In 1851, this journal was succeeded by the *Journal of Association,* which endured for six months. To the *Christian Socialist,* Kingsley contributed "thirty-nine poems, articles or stories"; to the *Journal of Association,* he "contributed only three poems and one article."[38] Kingsley's favorite among his contributions was a series titled "Bible Politics," in which he set out to show democracy to be "the idea of the Bible and the cause of God."[39]

By the end of 1850, Kingsley had established a reputation. He was the author of a blank-verse play, two novels, poems, reviews, and political-theological essays. Foreign visitors had begun to request the opportunity of meeting him, and other writers, the Swedish Frederika Bremer and Alfred Tennyson, had visited at Eversley. He had also received an offer from Charles A. Dana of the *New York Tribune* to print a new novel.[40]

Throughout 1851, Kingsley contributed to Christian Socialist periodicals and engaged in the controversy that surrounded them. The movement itself as well as "the author of 'Alton Locke'" was attacked in the *Edinburgh Review* and in the *Quarterly Review,* and in June, following a sermon preached at St. John's Church, Fitzroy Square, London, Kingsley was publicly admonished by the rector for having preached a message characterized as dangerous and untrue. The sermon should have been no surprise: in it Kingsley asserted that systems of society which accumulate capital into the hands of a few, leaving the masses crushed under debt or virtual slavery, are contrary to the kingdom of God as preached by Jesus.[41]

Following attacks in the press which included a demand by the *Daily News* that the Bishop of London investigate Kingsley's clerical fitness, the bishop forbade him to preach in London. On July 5, the sermon in question appeared in print. Bishop Blomfield read the sermon, entertained Kingsley, and subsequently withdrew his prohibition.[42]

This controversy, coupled with the abuse which greeted the volume publication of *Yeast,* exhausted Kingsley and once again he set off in search of rest. This time, however, instead of going to the West Country, he accompanied his parents on a European tour.[43]

While working at his various tasks during 1851, Kingsley had begun planning a new novel, *Hypatia: or, New Foes with an Old Face.* With this novel, Kingsley turned from the troubles of contemporary England to those of fifth-century Alexandria, where, as the subtitle indicates, he thought he found correspondences between his own time and that earlier age. If 1852 marks a literary departure for him, turning as he did from "the condition of England question" to historical fiction, it marks a political departure as well. With the demise of the *Christian Socialist* in June 1852, carrying Parson Lot's last words and "Epicedium," a poem signed in his own name, Kingsley withdrew from active participation in Christian Socialist activities.

III *Recognition and Honors*

Kingsley's career through 1852 is dominated by his Christian Socialist activities. During the years 1852–1863, Kingsley became one of the representative men of the mid-Victorian period: historical novelist, professor of history, amateur scientist, jingoist patriot, and Protestant apologist.

As early as 1850, Kingsley had begun to prepare for the writing of his third novel. The result of his preparation took three major forms, each in some way an attack on Neo-Platonism: a Socratic dialogue titled *Phaethon: or Loose Thoughts for Loose Thinkers,* which set out to exhibit the weaknesses of "Emersonian pseudo-spiritualism" as taught by the American Professor Windrush; the novel *Hypatia; or, New Foes with an Old Face;* and four lectures delivered in Edinburgh, *Alexandria and Her Schools,* published in 1854. *Hypatia* began appearing in *Fraser's* in January 1852. By August, Kingsley was vowing to complete *Hypatia* and write no more novels; he would instead devote himself to poetry.[44] He had published a few poems already and had begun experimenting with hexameters. These experiments produced "Andromeda," admired at the time as the finest English poem in that form. Also during the summer of 1852, Kingsley composed "Saint Maura" and reminded Parker of a suggestion Parker had made some years before of publishing a volume of Kingsley's poems. Parker, however, worried that *Hypatia* was hurting *Fraser's,* was uninterested.[45]

In April 1853, the final installment of *Hypatia* appeared; later that year the novel was issued in two volumes. Attacks on the book from high churchmen, coupled with F. D. Maurice's difficulties at King's College in a dispute over the issue of eternal damnation, a dispute which cost Maurice his position there, hurt and angered Kingsley. *Hypatia* had been a demanding novel to write, and Maurice was his closest friend, the one man among his many correspondents whom he addressed as "my Master."[46]

Adding to Kingsley's problems in the autumn of 1853 was the breakdown of Fanny's health following a miscarriage. To help Fanny recuperate, the family spent the late autumn and the winter of that year on the seaside at Torquay. Kingsley was with them as much as his duties at Eversley permitted, walking his children along the shore while searching for specimens to send to the naturalist Philip Gosse, with whom he had recently become acquainted.[47]

Always fascinated by geology and zoology, Kingsley turned his seaside wanderings into descriptive prose with an article, "The Wonders of the Shore," published in the *North British Review* in November 1854. In 1855, he expanded the article into a book, *Glaucus; or, the Wonders of the Shore,* which enabled him to begin reviewing scientific studies as well as popular works on geology.[48]

But the vacation in Devonshire led to other, more directly literary benefits as well, for it placed him in the country once inhabited by Elizabethan adventurers. Kingsley had been reading Elizabethan historians and discussing the Elizabethan age with J. A. Froude in preparation for writing a review. Consequently, his imagination had been fired by accounts of the heroic spirit of the sixteenth century, which he felt contrasted sharply with the singularly unheroic tendencies in his own age.

In 1849, following his suppression of piracy and headhunting in
the Malayan archipelago, the Rajah Sir James Brooke had been
charged in the House of Commons with illegal activity and in-
humane treatment of the Dyaks.[49] Kingsley had been incensed by
this attack. He had also been troubled by the so-called "Papal Aggression" of 1850 and by the mismanagement of the Crimean War.
Kingsley's concern for the spirit of British soldiers in the Crimea
emerged directly in his anonymous tract *Brave Words for Brave
Soldiers*. It emerged metaphorically in *Westward Ho!* Reflecting on
the heroism of the Elizabethans, who had defeated Spain, and con-
templating the bungling of his own generation and the effect of that
bungling on the spirit of front-line soldiers, Kingsley was moved to
dedicate *Westward Ho!* to Rajah Brooke and to Bishop George A.
Selwyn, who established the Church of England in New Zealand, as
modern counterparts of the Elizabethan hero.[50] The novel was well
received by the English public, and, by 1856, both *Westward Ho!*
and *Glaucus* were selling well. Moreover, his latest book, *The
Heroes; or, Greek Fairy Tales for My Children* had appeared.[51]

In the autumn of 1856, the Kingsleys entertained American
guests. First came Harriet Beecher Stowe and her sister. Next came
a journalist, W. H. Hurlbert, who was writing abolitionist propaganda for the English press.[52] Kingsley's abolitionist sympathies
found expression in *Two Years Ago,* a novel set in 1854 but published in 1857. The American abolitionist cause occupies the subplot, which tells the story of a love-struck dilettante American's
pursuit across Europe of a beautiful quadroon former slave who is
pretending to be an Italian actress.

Early in 1858 John Parker finally published Kingsley's
Andromeda and Other Poems, bringing into one volume poetry
which had appeared earlier in periodicals and work, such as the
title poem, which had been written with volume publication in
mind. Although Kingsley believed he lacked the "discursive fancy"
necessary to make him a great poet, he was generally pleased both
with the poems and with their reception. Kingsley's own judgment
was that his poems and *Hypatia* were likely to be his lasting contribution to literature.[53]

In 1859, Kingsley attempted to write another historical novel,
this time on the Pilgrimage of Grace, an uprising in the northern
counties in England in 1536 against the Protestant Reformation
begun by Henry VIII. The climax of the movement occurred in
Yorkshire, where Robert Aske, supported by some 30,000 men,

captured York and demanded the return of England to papal obedience and the establishment of a Parliament free of royal influence. Eventually, Aske, tricked into believing his cause had been won, surrendered himself and his men. He and 220 to 250 of his men were executed in 1537. Kingsley completed his preliminary research, including a trip to Yorkshire for background materials, and he managed to write sections of the novel and to send them to Macmillan. But he was unable to complete the work, which his daughter Mary eventually finished and published in 1916 under the title *The Tutor's Story.*[54] He also rejected an offer to join a group of friends in writing a series of "historical sketches of English heroes for boys" and satisfied himself with writing reviews and with puffing *Tom Brown's Schooldays,* published by his friend Thomas Hughes.[55]

However, 1859 did not pass without moment for Kingsley. In this year, he began to receive official recognition. He was now an historical novelist of considerable stature, a poet, a prominent Protestant apologist, a science buff of some reputation, and one of the leading parsons of his time. On May 7, largely because of Prince Albert's appreciation of *The Saint's Tragedy* and *Two Years Ago,* Kingsley was offered the appointment of Chaplain to the Queen.[56] According to Fanny, royal favor brought to her husband a welcome change in the attitude of the press: "Though he still waged war as heretofore against bigotry, ignorance, and intolerance, and was himself unchanged, the attacks on him from outside were less frequent and less bitter."[57]

In 1860, royal favor was his again when on May 9, probably at Prince Albert's suggestion, Kingsley was offered the Professorship of Modern History at Cambridge. More parson than historian, Kingsley was popular with his students if not with other historians outside his own circle. It was this popularity and Kingsley's interest in his students which once again appealed to the Prince Consort. In 1861, the Prince of Wales was sent to Cambridge, where Kingsley was made his tutor in history. When Prince Albert died later that year, however, the Prince of Wales was withdrawn from Cambridge. Soon after, the young prince named Kingsley his chaplain.[58]

Early in 1862, Kingsley, at home and returning to his parish duties, was reminded by Fanny over breakfast one morning that "'Rose, Maurice, and Mary have got their book *[The Heroes],* and baby must have his.'"[59] According to Fanny, Kingsley arose without a reply, locked himself in his study, and within a half-hour emerged with the first chapter of *The Water-Babies: A Fairy Tale for a Land Baby*.[60] In this tale of spiritual renewal, Kingsley drew on his knowledge of biology and geology, combining evolutionary theories with theology and mixing both with the revelations of the Children's Employment Commission of 1861.[61] The result is Kingsley's most imaginative book.

By the 1860s, Kingsley possessed a national reputation and was the recipient of royal favor. Nevertheless, his troubles with the High-Church party were far from over. They were, in fact, about to become critical. Although the publication in 1861 of *Essays and Reviews* had disturbed many English clergymen, Kingsley had remained steady. He was angered, however, in February of 1863 by the treatment Maurice continued to receive over his disavowal of eternal damnation.[62] Maintaining public silence, Kingsley confined his support of Maurice to personal letters, one of which congratulated his friend on a victory over Dr. Pusey in an argument conducted in letters to *The Times*.[63]

Nevertheless, the friendship of Maurice and Kingsley was well known and not even Kingsley's public silence in the dispute between Pusey and Maurice could alleviate the intensity of Pusey's disfavor. In the summer of 1863, the Prince of Wales attended the Oxford Commemoration and suggested that Kingsley receive the D.C.L. degree. Other Oxford men supported the proposal, but Pusey, leading the High-Church party, opposed him on the grounds that he was the author of immoral books, singling out *Hypatia* as the most profligate and doctrinally false. Upset by the controversy, Kingsley had his name withdrawn. Years later, some Oxford friends suggested another attempt; he declined, stating that until the charge of immorality had been withdrawn from his novel he could not consider it. In 1866, when asked to preach a series of Lenten sermons at Oxford, he refused for the same reason.[64] But if one honor was denied in 1863, another was accorded when Sir Charles Bunbury proposed and Sir Charles Lyell seconded his admission as a Fellow of the Geological Society.[65]

IV *Kingsley vs. Newman*

The end of 1863 found Kingsley ill once more. As Fanny said, his physical condition was "a bad preparation for the storm of controversy which burst upon [him] and which eventually produced Dr. Newman's famous 'Apologia pro vita sua.'"[66] For years, Kingsley had attacked the Roman Church, had opposed nearly everything Newman had come to stand for, and had himself been attacked by the High-Church party. On the other hand, Newman had been the target of bias and innuendo since before his conversion to Catholicism. After his conversion, he had come to represent for Kingsley "all that was fascinating, elegant, perverse, and spurious in Roman Catholicism."[67]

In the January 1864 issue of *Macmillan's Magazine,* Charles Kingsley, Cambridge Professor of Modern History and Chaplain to the Queen and to the Prince of Wales, commented in a review of Froude's *History of England,* volumes VII and VIII, that

truth, for its own sake, had never been a virtue with the Roman clergy. Father Newman informs us that it need not, and on the whole ought not to be; that cunning is the weapon which Heaven has given to the saints wherewith to withstand the brute male force of the wicked world which marries and is given in marriage. Whether his notion be doctrinally correct or not, it is at least historically so.[68]

Thus began a dispute which produced the greatest spiritual autobiography of the nineteenth century and tied Kingsley's name forever to the controversy which has most seriously damaged his reputation.

Briefly, the facts of the conflict are as follows. In December 1863, an unidentified person sent Newman a copy of the January 1864 issue of *Macmillan's Magazine* with the offending passage marked in pencil. On December 30, 1863, Newman wrote a letter to Macmillan, objecting to the "slander."[69] On January 6, 1864, Kingsley wrote to Newman, informing him that he had seen the previous letter and identifying the document to which he had referred as Newman's sermon "Wisdom and Innocence," published in 1844 as No. XX in *Sermons on Subjects of the Day.* On being shown that he had misinterpreted Newman, Kingsley offered to "retract my accusation as publicly as I have made it."[70] In his reply on January 7, Newman expressed his amazement that Kingsley was the author of the offending remarks and called to his attention the fact that the sermon had dealt with "the bearing of the Christian towards the world, and of the character of the reaction of that bearing upon him."[71] Events were further complicated by a mysterious correspondent known as "X. Y.," whose letter of January 5 Newman answered on January 8. In his letter, Newman denied knowing that Kingsley was the author of the slander, briefly reviewed his troubles since 1833, and became increasingly indignant at the suggestion that proof of his innocence rested with him. He insisted that Kingsley either prove his point or state the impossibility of so doing. He did not want the matter smoothed over or explained. On January 10, he added a note that he regarded his correspondence with Kingsley to be public property.

The next round began on January 14, when Kingsley wrote to say he had seen both X. Y.'s letter and Newman's reply. He enclosed a copy of his retraction. On January 17, Newman responded. He asserted that the retraction was likely to mislead the public into believing "that I have been confronted with definite extracts from my works, and have laid before you my own interpretations of them. Such a proceeding I have indeed challenged, but have not been so fortunate as to bring about."[72] In reply to Newman, Kingsley, on January 18, asserted that the British public would not misunderstand his retraction, but expressed his willingness to omit two passages which "may, however, be open to such a bad use."[73] Having done that, he said he had done "as much as one English gentleman can expect from another."[74] On January 22, Newman wrote to Macmillan, summarizing the controversy between himself and Kingsley, and expressing his dissatisfaction with the proposed retraction on the same grounds as he had stated to his adversary.

In the February issue, *Macmillan's Magazine* carried Kingsley's retraction, the key passage of which follows:

Dr. Newman has by letter expressed, in the strongest terms, his denial of the meaning which I have put upon his words. It only remains, therefore, for me to express my hearty regret at having so seriously mistaken him.[75]

What Newman objected to is that without identifying specific passages in the sermon "Wisdom and Innocence" Kingsley left it to be inferred that the meaning he found was a perfectly natural one to find, and furthermore, that it was Newman's "interpretation" which had revealed his error to him. Newman insisted that he had not made the original statement in the first place.

The last exchange began when Newman published *Mr. Kingsley and Dr. Newman: A Correspondence on the Question Whether Dr. Newman Teaches that Truth Is No Virtue?* This pamphlet contained the correspondence summarized above with the addition of a witty and sarcastic section titled "Reflections on the Above."

Without the publication of this pamphlet, it is possible that the whole affair would have ended.[76] In response to it, however, Kinglsey failed out in his pamphlet *"What, Then, Does Dr. Newman Mean?" A Reply to a Pamphlet Lately Published by Dr. Newman*. In his rejoinder, Kingsley struck not just at the literal truth of a specific sermon, but charged Newman with having lived a dishonest life.

By this point in the dispute, both men were exhausted. Kingsley attempted to relax, hoping that Newman would not reply. He was wrong. *Apologia pro Vita Sua: Being a Reply to a Pamphlet Entitled "What, Then, Does Dr. Newman Mean?"* began to appear weekly as a series of pamphlets. While Newman wrote his *Apologia* in a state perilously near nervous collapse, J. A. Froude persuaded Kingsley to accompany him to the Continent. Kingsley himself did not reply to Newman, nor did Newman respond to the Rev. Frederick Meyrick's anticlimactic pamphlet *But Is Not Kingsley Right, After All?*[77]

The tempers of the two men cooled following the publication of the *Apologia*, and, although neither sought the other's company, a kind of conciliation was reached between them. Beginning in 1865, Newman withdrew from the *Apologia* all of the sections which attacked Kingsley personally, and eventually declared that his anger had been a rhetorical guise necessary for gaining a sympathetic hearing from the British public.[78] In 1868, Kingsley wrote to Sir W. E. Cope that he had read Newman's poem "Dream of Gerontius" with "awe and admiration."[79] When Newman heard of Kingsley's death in 1875, he said a Mass for his soul.[80]

V *Last Works and Renown*

From a modern perspective, the debate with Newman is probably the most interesting event in Kingsley's life during the 1860s. During this decade, however, he was involved in other matters as well. In 1862, he wrote to Sir Charles Bunbury declaring his intention of lecturing on the "American Question" during the October term.[81] In 1864, he published *The Roman and the Teuton*, a collection of his Cambridge history lectures. In spite of his earlier abolitionist sympathies, expressed in *Two Years Ago*, by this time Kingsley was a supporter of the South as an hereditary aristocracy. He believed blacks to be incapable of self-government and believed that once the South was free from the North it would be amenable to English influence and that the South would thus be forced to treat the blacks better.[82]

In the summer of 1865, Kingsley entertained at Eversley the young widow Queen Emma of the Sandwich Islands. Evidently his awe of royalty overcame his racial attitudes, for Fanny's letters reveal that she and her husband were captivated by Emma. But his antipathy toward nonwhite races emerged again in 1866 when Edward John Eyre, governor of Jamaica, was investigated by a Royal Commission. In October 1865, Eyre had put down a rebellion by killing or executing more than 600 natives in one month.[83] In England, the inquiry caused the formation of the Jamaica Committee, which wished Eyre to be prosecuted for murder, and of the Eyre Defense Fund. Kingsley joined the latter, thereby cutting himself off from his old friends John Ludlow and Thomas Hughes, who took the other side.[84]

Also in 1865, Kingsley published his final novel. *Hereward, the Last of the English* appeared serially in *Good Words* from January through December of that year. In 1866, Macmillan published the novel in two volumes as *Hereward the Wake, "Last of the English."* Kingsley tried to write other novels, but he was unable to get them started. In 1866, he proposed to Macmillan a story to be called *Darling, the History of a Wise Woman,* but was unable to write it. In 1868, he proposed another, a novel or romance, to Macmillan, but once again nothing came of it.[85]

Briefly in 1867, Kingsley took over from Froude the editorship of *Fraser's.* As temporary editor, he attempted to attract scientific articles.[86] But controversy was never far away, and during the year attacks on Kingsley's Cambridge professorship increased. The pressure mounted, and Kingsley, who had never felt secure as an academic, finally resigned in 1869.[87]

As Kingsley tried to write another novel, edited *Fraser's,* and worried over his professorship, he managed to write for children a series of articles on science. Published originally in *Good Words for the Young* from November 1868 through October 1869, *Madam How and Lady Why* was issued in 1870 with the subtitle *First Lessons in Earth Lore for Children.* In 1869, approximately four months after he had resigned his Cambridge professorship, Kingsley was appointed Canon of Chester. In November he was installed, and in December he and his daughter Rose sailed for the West Indies.[88]

Kingsley had yearned for this trip for nearly a lifetime. While there, he traveled extensively, visiting the places his mother had described, and keeping notes on the vegetation. Always adept at writing descriptive prose, he contributed "Letters from the Tropics" to *Good Words*. When he returned home, he published them in 1871 as *At Last: A Christmas in the West Indies*. In Chester in May 1870, Kingsley communicated his interest in science to his new associates by helping to organize what became the Chester Natural History Society. In 1872, he dedicated his book *Town Geology* to his classes in Chester, and because of his enthusiasm for science was made President of the Midland Institute in Birmingham.[89]

Aging, and beginning to receive the sort of recognition that would have made his life easier had it been granted earlier, Kingsley resigned his canonry at Chester to accept an appointment to a vacant stall in Westminster Abbey.[90] Also in 1873, he published *Prose Idylls, New and Old*.

Advised by his doctors in 1873 to take a sea voyage for his health, Kingsley, accompanied by Rose, sailed for North America on January 29, 1874. Although he was supposed to rest, he took lectures along and traveled in the United States and Canada for six months. In the process he met a number of notable Americans: William Cullen Bryant, Henry Ward Beecher, Longfellow, Asa Gray, Twain, Whittier, and Oliver Wendell Holmes.[91]

However much he enjoyed his trip, it tired him. In San Francisco a cold he had caught earlier, in Niagara, became worse, causing a change of plans that took him to Denver and Colorado Springs in June. On July 14, he wrote to Fanny, longing to be home. By the time he returned to his duties at Westminster Abbey about three weeks later, his health was unimproved. Late in November, bothered by a bad lung and other related complaints of his own, as well as by the collapse of Fanny's health, he caught a cold again. On December 3, he took Fanny home to Eversley, where she suffered a relapse and seemed about to die. He nursed her himself until on December 28 he was in bed with pneumonia. On January 23, 1875, he died.[92]

CHAPTER 2

A Play: The Saint's Tragedy

IN 1842, after leaving Cambridge and before beginning his curacy, Kingsley began writing a prose biography of St. Elizabeth of Hungary. The biography was to be illustrated, unpublished, and presented as a wedding gift to Fanny, whom Kingsley had won from Puseyism. Before it was well underway, though, Kingsley projected another

work of the same kind . . . — a life of St Theresa — as a specimen of the dreamy mystic, in contrast with the working ascetic St Elizabeth, and to contrast the celibate saint with the married one.[1]

He neither completed the one nor began the other. In 1844, the Kingsleys were married, and Charles began turning his biography of St. Elizabeth into a blank-verse closet drama. Kingsley's use of the life of St. Elizabeth to illustrate the "fatal 'Manichean' tendencies implicit in the Roman practice of celibacy"[2] survived the transition from prose history to blank-verse drama. All that remains of the biography are a rambling attack on the twin evils of celibacy and monasticism and the sexually suggestive illustrations.[3]

By the summer of 1847, the play had been completed and Kingsley was being advised by Frederick Denison Maurice and a group of other friends to publish it.[4] In 1848, *The Saint's Tragedy* with a preface by Maurice appeared through

the heroic magnanimity of Mr. J[ohn] Parker, West Strand, who, though a burnt child, does not dread the fire. No one else would have it.[5]

Elizabeth, a scrupulous Catholic and the daughter of the King of Hungary, was affianced at birth to Lewis, the Landgrave of Thuringia. As her wedding day approaches, Elizabeth is confused by the conflict between her wish to marry Lewis and the Church's

32

teaching that celibacy is the highest state to which she can aspire.

In spite of her misgivings, Elizabeth marries Lewis, with whom she might have lived a happy and useful life. But at this critical moment she and Lewis submit themselves to the rule of the monk Conrad of Marpurg, who becomes their confessor. Conrad, whose consuming ambition is to train a saint, is drawn to Elizabeth. Conrad's regimen for Elizabeth's training consists mainly of denying her all normal outlets for her strong natural affections. First, Conrad parts Elizabeth from Lewis by enlisting him in a crusade; Lewis dies of a fever on the way. Next, Conrad separates Elizabeth from her children, and then, on the grounds that her charity is an indulgence in selfish pleasure, he eventually denies her even her ministry to the poor. Finally, he obtains for the Church the remainder of her wealth. Impoverished, virtually isolated, and exhausted by self-denial and self-chastisement, Elizabeth dies with a purposely ambiguous deathbed utterance on her lips:

> Now I must sleep — for ere the sun shall rise,
> I must be gone upon a long, long journey
> To him I love.
>
> *Con.* She means her heavenly Bridegroom —
> The Spouse of souls.
>
> *Eliz.* I said, to him I love . . . . (IV, iv)

As Elizabeth "folds herself into an attitude of repose," Conrad is satisfied that he has made a saint, but is nagged by the fear that his training has smirched something fine:

> The work is done! Diva Elizabeth!
> And I have trained one saint before I die!
> Yet now 'tis done, is't well done? On my lips
> Is triumph: but what echo in my heart?
> Alas! the inner voice is sad and dull,
> Even at the crown and shout of victory.
>
> (V, ii)

Shortly thereafter, Conrad is killed by a mob avenging the death of their relatives at the hands of his heresy-hunting agents.

The Saint's Tragedy received mixed reviews. The most hostile came from High-Churchmen and their sympathizers, who objected to Kingsley's representation of the medieval Church. One such writer for the *English Review,* commenting that the play had merits and that it would "secure its author's fame," identified what were to become Kingsley's characteristic faults: "exaggeration, an overstrained boldness verging upon coarseness, a tendency to bitterness and occasional bursts of fine talk." Furthermore, he observed, Kingsley "understated the ascetic argument and overstated the ascetic aberration."[6]

But if this review identifies Kingsley's characteristic faults, *The Saint's Tragedy* itself establishes the major themes that Kingsley treated throughout his literary life: the glorification of marriage and the sanctity of the family, the ennobling influence of woman, the importance of serving the poor in brotherhood, and what came to be called, despite Kingsley's objections, muscular Christianity.[7]

Kingsley's central concern in *The Saint's Tragedy* is to assert the naturalness and the goodness of love between the sexes and to locate the fulfillment of that love in marriage. Kingsley's belief in the world as the outward expression of God and in the flesh as the outward expression of the soul led him to accept man's instincts and sexual nature as God-given. Through their frank acceptance of their sexual nature, men and women marry and bear children; through their love of each other, men and women understand the love of God for His church; and through their love of their children, they understand the fatherhood of God. Because, for Kingsley, marriage is the state through which God most fully reveals Himself, it, not celibacy, is the highest state to which men and women can aspire.[8] For Kingsley, as for the Victorians generally, the family was sacred. From Kingsley's point of view, therefore, ascetism is an aberration whose suppression of the sexual element of human nature leads to a false conception of God and eventually to fanaticism.

In the play, Elizabeth's instinctual acceptance of her natural impulses conflicts with the Church's emphasis on asceticism. By denying Elizabeth all normal outlets for her natural affections, Conrad subdues a noble and passionate woman to a life based on false principles. For Conrad, Elizabeth is a saint because she transcends the world, which hides the glory of God. For Kingsley, she is a saint because, martyred to his notion of Roman Catholic orthodoxy, she stands as a warning to the nineteenth century not to go and do likewise.

Act II clearly establishes Elizabeth's dilemma. Taught by the

Church that the ascetic life is the holy life, Elizabeth is torn between that lesson and her natural desires. In Act II, Scene i, Elizabeth, unable to sleep, considers her problem: Is love for both Lewis and Christ contradictory? She loves her husband, but she has been taught that

> . . . love is of the flesh,
> And that's our house-bred foe, the adder in our bosoms.

According to the Church, Elizabeth's love for Lewis is a "snare." But Elizabeth *feels* differently. As she gazes from the window, she visualizes nature as "one vast bride-bed." Lewis awakens and remonstrates with Elizabeth for having scourged herself in order to subdue her flesh. For the moment, Elizabeth abandons theological questions and returns to bed promising to

> stop those wise lips with a kiss,
> And lead thee back to scenes of simpler bliss.

By Act II, Scene ix, five years have passed since the wedding. Although Lewis accepts marriage as sacred, Elizabeth, influenced by Conrad, remains troubled. Lewis warmly confides to Elizabeth that on their wedding day he "slipped from time into eternity." For him, marriage is "the life-long miracle," a state of innocence akin to that of Eden in which

> the spirit and the flesh
> Are one again, and new-born souls walk free,
> And name in mystic language all things new,
> Naked, and not ashamed.

Swept up by her inner conviction of the miraculous nature of marriage, Elizabeth echoes her husband:

> Lewis, I am too happy! floating higher
> Than e'er my will had dared to soar, though able;
> But circumstance, which is the will of God,
> Beguiled my cowardice to that, which, daring,
> I found most natural, when I feared it most.
> Love would have had no strangeness in mine eyes, —
> Save from the prejudice which others taught me —
> They should know best. Yet now this wedlock seems

A second infancy's baptismal robe,
A heaven, my spirit's antenatal home,
Lost in blind pining girlhood — found now, found!

Nevertheless, in the aside which follows this admission that her impulses may be more trustworthy than Conrad's teaching, Elizabeth's doubts return: "What have I said? Do I blaspheme? Alas!" At the end of the scene, Elizabeth cries out at her confessor that loving her husband has not made her less holy and that Conrad has poisoned all her joys "with foulest scruples" and shown her "nameless sins." Conrad in turn charges that her outburst proves she is the captive of "passions unsanctified, and carnal leanings." The scene ends with Elizabeth collapsed and sobbing.

Related to Kingsley's belief that marriage is the natural, God-ordained consequence of love is his belief that through love and marriage man discovers his vocation. Kingsley develops this theme through his portrayal of Lewis.

At the beginning of the play, Lewis is a knight whose passive strength needs a spark to make it active. In Act I, Scene ii, Lewis declares to Conrad and Walter of Varila that he does not dread "toil," for "toil" is "the true knight's pastime." Lewis's problem is that in a world full of life "whose heart goes out a-Maying all the year," he lacks a fixed and intense will:

> . . . in my fitful thought
> What skill is there, to turn my faith to sight —
> To pierce blank Heaven, like some trained falconer
> After his game, beyond all human ken?

The two counselors, the ascetic Conrad and the manly Walter, offer contrasting advice to Lewis.

Conrad insists that Lewis should dedicate himself either to "peerless Mary" or to one of the other female saints. According to him, such devotion would free his spirit and send matter "transubstantiate to heaven." Love for a female saint is, Conrad says, "Love's heaven, without its hell; the golden fruit/Without the foul husk . . . . " Conrad's piety is, however, Walter's poison. Walter's more earthy advice is that visions of matter transubstantiate, such as Conrad preaches, are the product of "an indigestion,"

> . . . male hysterics, by starvation bred
> And huge conceit.

Unlike Conrad, Walter admits no duality in creation and insists on the spiritual necessity of frankly accepting one's manhood.

> Will you be cozened, Sir, by these air-blown fancies . . . ?
> Cast off God's gift of manhood,
> And, like the dog in the adage, drop the true bone
> With snapping at the sham one in the water?
> What were you born a man for?

Asserting that he cannot live on a dream, that he requires a flesh and blood woman from whom

> To learn my daily task; — in her pure eyes
> To see the living type of those heaven-glories
> I dare not look on . . . .

Walter leads Lewis to think of Elizabeth. Once married, Lewis acknowledges Elizabeth as his spiritual guide and discovers through marriage a timeless, spaceless world unknown before and unattainable except through marriage.

Developing the theme of the sanctity of love and marriage is clearly Kingsley's central concern. Seeing it in *The Saint's Tragedy* prepares us for its later appearance in the novels. Another theme which appears first in *The Saint's Tragedy* and then more importantly later, especially in *Yeast* and *Alton Locke*, is the importance of serving the poor in brotherhood. In *The Saint's Tragedy*, the impulse for service originates in two sources: first in Elizabeth's innate compassion and, second, in social problems perceived by Kingsley to correspond to those that occupied his mind throughout the 1840s.

Elizabeth's compassion for the poor is aroused as soon as she becomes aware of their condition. In Act II, Scene iv, Elizabeth returns from a walk through the streets where she had gone dressed roughly in order to remain anonymous. Her comments reveal a Kingsleyan view of the condition of Thuringia/England:

> We sit in a cloud, and sing, like pictured angels,
> And say, the world runs smooth — while right below
> Welters the black fermenting heap of life
> On which our state is built . . . .

Momentarily chided by her nurse, Elizabeth details the particular distresses she has seen:

> I turned into an alley 'neath the wall —
> And stepped from earth to hell. — The light of heaven,
> The common air, was narrow, gross, and dun;
> The tiles did drop from the eaves; the unhinged doors
> Tottered o'er inky pools, where reeked and curdled
> The offal of a life; the gaunt-haunched swine
> Growled at their christened playmates o'er the scraps.
> Shrill mothers cursed; wan children wailed; sharp coughs
> Rang through the crazy chambers; hungry eyes
> Glared dumb reproach, and old perplexity,
> Too stale for words; o'er still and webless looms
> The listless craftsmen through their elf-locks scowled;
> These were my people!

It is not far from this description to *Yeast* and *Alton Locke*.

Elizabeth's opinion of the condition of Thuringia's poor is supported and made to seem contemporary by references to the Corn Laws in Act II, Scene vii, and to Victorian economic issues in Act II, Scene viii. In Act II, Scene vii, Elizabeth, standing at the top of a flight of stairs, is besieged by a mob screaming for bread. From below, a merchant, accompanied by Walter of Varila, enters with a cartload of wheat. With the supply down, the merchant refuses to sell his wheat for less than three times its normal value:

> I bought it on speculation — I must live —
> I get my bread by buying corn that's cheap,
> And selling where 'tis dearest. Mass, you need it,
> And you must pay according to your need.

The merchant praises Elizabeth as one who will protect trade. Elizabeth reproaches him for being coldhearted and for increasing his profit by preying on the misery of the poor. A more direct solution is found by Walter, who mounts the wagon and throws the grain to the people, promising to pay the market price and to allow the merchant to take out the rest in room and board in the castle dungeon.

In Act II, Scene viii, Victorian *laissez-faire* attitudes are expressed by a group of nobles who, in discussing the condition of Thuringia, employ the standard Victorian interpretation of the

Malthusian arguments concerning the relationship between population and food supply. Overpopulation and a low supply of food has
caused a famine. Elizabeth has responded by distributing grain
from the Landgrave's holdings. Count Hugo believes that such
charity only aggravates the problem by encouraging the poor to
marry and breed. The Abbot believes that Elizabeth's charity interferes with heaven's chastenings: without Elizabeth's interference
the famine would have reduced the population and sped their souls
to heaven. Another nobleman adds that Elizabeth's interference has
encouraged to remain in Thuringia those who had planned to emigrate. In this conversation, the nobles present three versions of the
standard Victorian argument against charity: charity works against
nature by encouraging an increase of population during times of
want, by preventing the reduction of the population through starvation, and by discouraging a greater distribution of population
through emigration.

As a solution to the woes of Thuringia, these nobles propose a
social equilibrium reached by allowing nature to balance itself.
Count Hugo observes that a sharp famine reduces population and
raises prices. The more he earns, the more he can spend. Thus,
money circulates, eventually reaching the lower classes and bene-
fiting all. This view is sanctioned by the Church when the Abbot
notes that it is "the self-interest of each . . . which produces in the
aggregate the happy equilibrium of all." Left alone, nature will
right itself and create the proper relationship between population,
food supply, and money.[9]

In the next stage of the discussion, Walter of Varila speaks for
Kingsley in condemning the *laissez-faire* attitudes of the other
nobles. Walter agrees with the others that alms are a "badge of
slavery" and that the poor should be taught independence. He believes, however, that the poor should be put "not out of the reach,
but out of the need, of charity." The Abbot responds that the
result of alms-giving is idleness, deceit, and immorality; privation
teaches "the need of self-exertion," and misery proves "the fool-
ishness of crime." Arguing that one cannot teach the poor to be
men by treating them as brutes, Walter suggests that if the working
classes are idle and immoral they learned to be so from watching
the nobles.

To substantiate this position, Walter reports a sermon he has
heard recently on a subject dear to Thomas Carlyle and Kingsley:
the idle aristocracy. The working classes cannot respect religion

when they see their betters growing fat on church lands, neglecting sacraments, trading in benefices, and regarding the ministry as "lumber-room" wherein to stow away the unwanted of their own class. But if religion has lost respect through its abuses, the court has corrupted the working classes by housing them worse than horses. Walter asserts that the nobility have created the condition of the poor and now seek to gloss over the result with an appeal to "natural law" and greedy self-interest. He implicitly predicts a revolution. Clearly Walter's condemnation of the idle aristocracy and his raising of the specter of revolution places *The Saint's Tragedy* in the tradition of Carlyle's *Past and Present* and places it more firmly in the 1840s than in the 1220s. Having placed nineteenth-century social and economic problems in a medieval setting, Kingsley moved to the contemporary scene where in his Christian Socialist activities and in his first two novels, *Yeast* and *Alton Locke,* he considered solutions.

The last of the major themes to appear in *The Saint's Tragedy* and to persist throughout Kingsley's career is that of muscular Christianity. This theme is treated primarily through the character of Walter and through the obvious contrast of Walter with Conrad. Walter does what Kingsleyan muscular Christians do: he takes a plain, straightforward, common-sense approach to life; he affirms the goodness of man's sexual nature and revels in a life of action; he opposes the feminine weakness of Roman Catholic asceticism, and, without quite thumping his chest, celebrates his manhood. A practical, pragmatic man of affairs, Walter is the bluff, hearty type that finds fuller expression in Lancelot Smith *(Yeast),* Tom Thurnall *(Two Years Ago),* and Amyas Leigh *(Westward Ho!).*

Conrad denies what Walter affirms and through his exploiting of whatever will further his ends becomes the type of Roman Catholic sneak whose regard for truth is "sophisticated" away by "Jesuitry." This type also finds its fuller expression later in Lancelot's cousin Luke *(Yeast),* in Eustace Leigh *(Westward Ho!),* and in Kingsley's interpretation of the character of John Henry Newman. By placing Conrad and Walter side by side, heightening the weakness of the one by contrast with the manly strength of the other, Kingsley not only emphasized the values of "muscular Christianity" but also hit on a fictional device he would employ for the rest of his career.

CHAPTER 3

Novels of Social Purpose

YEAST (1848), *Alton Locke* (1850), and *Two Years Ago* (1857)
are directly concerned with the plight of the laboring poor and
with the contemporary scene. Indeed, the first two novels emerge
directly from Kingsley's Christian Socialist activities and, like the
"Condition of England" novels of Benjamin Disraeli, Elizabeth
Gaskell, Charles Dickens, Frances Trollope, and Charlotte Brontë,
they reflect life among the poor during the "hungry" and stormy
1840s. The third novel marks a return to the contemporary scene,
but focuses more sharply than the first two on the subjects of sanitation and public health. Understanding these three books, however, presupposes an acquaintance with Kingsley's social attitudes.

I *Kingsley and Christian Socialism*

Although the Christian Socialist movement has attracted considerable attention and is an important development in nineteenth-
century social history, I will be concerned here only with Kingsley's
involvement. His participation in Christian Socialist activities
began in 1848 and ended when the *Journal of Association* ceased
publication in 1852. From then on, he became increasingly Tory
and paternalistic.

The basis for Kingsley's Christian Socialism is to be found in the
belief of the theologian Frederick Denison Maurice that the earth is
the Kingdom of Christ and that the Universal Church is society in
its perfect form.[1] For Kingsley, as for Maurice, Christianity is not
ascetic; it does not provide an escape from life and the problems of
the day. Instead, it is actively concerned with life, liberating and
freeing men by causing them to acknowledge the reality of God and
the society revealed by God through the Bible. Thus, Kingsley emphasized the interdependence of social, political, and religious
beliefs.

Kingsley's faith in this interdependence derives from his view of the relationship between man's "natural affections," his instincts, and Christianity. Because the higher natural law is the law of God, man's instincts are good and, more often than not, reliable guides for conduct. A man loves a woman, a mother loves her child: these are natural impulses which are both good and healthy. They should not be denied, for denying the instincts leads to asceticism and celibacy. This, in turn, produces a passive response to life akin to opium or alcohol in obtaining peace of mind. Therefore, a religion that preaches denial of the natural affections corrupts its adherents. But if one can err by denying his instincts, he can also err by indiscriminately indulging them and becoming bestial.

What Kingsley needed was an escape from the apparent dilemma of being forced to choose between asceticism, the unnatural rejection of instinct, and bestiality, surrender to instinct. His interpretation of Christianity provided him with such an escape by suggesting to him the idea of the "artificial" man, man as he should be and can be if he will place his instinct at the service of an ideal. Because the higher law of nature, the law of God, has descended to man in the form of Christian morals, man can submit his instinct to them, curb his bestiality, and thereby create an "artificial" man, who is the sort of man he *should* be. Sanctified by Christian morality, the natural affection of a man for a woman raises and ennobles man. Instinct thus sanctified becomes expressible in monogamous marriage, producing a family, an ideal unit created by man in accordance with Christian morality. In marriage, the "artificial" man is delivered from both the bondage of bestiality and the unnaturalness of celibacy. He labors for his family and united with them he discovers self-fulfillment. Kingsley's social action springs from his personal morality.

The "artificial" man looks about him and observes that the working classes live in squalor and disease. His natural affections are engaged and, enlightened by a vision of social justice provided by Christian morality, he dismisses as inadequate the mechanical, competitive, individualizing creed of *laissez-faire* political economy. Man can, if he will, create through legislation an "artificial" society, the sort of society he *should* have. For example, man need not suffer the ravages of preventable and curable diseases if he will join with others and apply his scientific knowledge to the creation of proper living conditions. Society can clean streets, build adequate sewers, and provide clean water. In other words, man can raise his living conditions above the bestial by creating an "artificial" society.

Improving his economic condition is, however, more problematical. Early in the nineteenth century men accepted poverty as inevitable and supported charity instead of reform as a way of dealing with it. But just as science showed disease to be preventable or curable, so industry promised work for all.[2] The principle of *laissez-faire*, however, tended to isolate men from each other in a competitive system. The effect was, as viewed by Kingsley as well as by Thomas Carlyle (an important influence here), the dehumanization of the English working class through the mechanical operation of economic laws, or, in other words, the substitution of cash values for human values.

David Ricardo and his followers taught that the rate of wages depends primarily upon the supply of workers and the demand for their labor; only decreases in population or increases in capital can raise the general rate of wages.[3] According to this prevailing theory, each laborer competes against the others for work, driving wages down as the number of laborers increases. In effect, poverty and disease serve to regulate the numbers of the poor in competition. So regarded, too vigorous an intervention in the operation of this system only compounds the problem by increasing the supply of workers and by consequently decreasing the amount of available capital needed for the business expansion which alone causes an increased demand for labor. The Manchester School of economics, with which Ricardo is linked, described a system but did not conceive a society.

Kingsley rejected the tendency he found among the Radicals of the 1840s to separate social and political beliefs from their religious roots. He also rejected labor unions on the grounds that they were competitive and that their only real weapon — the strike — was ineffective. Trade unionists sought to organize in order to compete within the Manchester system. But, according to Ricardo's theory of wages, which Kingsley seems to have accepted, strikes could not permanently raise the general rate of wages.[4] Therefore, Kingsley believed the competitiveness of the unions led to social chaos and to no real economic gain.

Nevertheless, Kingsley thought that workers could help themselves, temporarily at least, by organizing cooperatives. By working together instead of against each other, the workers would form a community which would share instead of compete.

Through his sermons, tracts, and novels, Kingsley sought to awaken to its duty a group Carlyle in *Past and Present* had termed the "Idle Aristocracy." He attempted to convince both the aristocrat and the worker that the only hope for social regeneration lay in a moral reform of individuals that expressed itself in the recognition of responsibilities to a society "of organically related members bound together by sympathy and corporate feeling."[5] He proposed, in short, a society which emphasized the interconnectedness of social, political, and religious beliefs.[6]

Kingsley's first two novels, *Yeast* and *Alton Locke,* are attempts to awaken the slumbering social conscience of the upper classes and thereby to begin the restoration of society. In *Two Years Ago,* he assesses the progress made and focuses on the particular problems of sanitation and public health. In doing so, he develops once again the recurring Victorian theme of the redemptive nature of work.

II Yeast

Lancelot Smith, the protagonist, is a spiritually unsettled young man with an income of two thousand a year and no vocation. At the country estate of Squire Lavington, Lancelot becomes acquainted with a group that includes the Squire's daughters Argemone and Honoria; Colonel Bracebridge, a talented but idle man; Lord Minchampstead, a man generous to the limits proscribed by mammonism; Lord Vieuxbois, a representative of Young England; Claude and Sabina Mellot, artists; and Tregarva, the gamekeeper. Among Lancelot's city relatives are his banker uncle and Luke, a Tractarian cousin.

The two daughters form an obvious contrast: Argemone is High Church and intellectual, spending her time among books, statuettes, and dried flowers; Honoria is full of "wild simple passion" and charitably assists the poor and ill. Falling in love with Argemone at first glance, Lancelot must win her from asceticism. During their conversations, Lancelot sets his arguments against the weakness of her feminine intellect, and her womanhood eventually surrenders to the "energy of his manly will" (XV, p. 142). After this, she experiences the "delicious feeling of being utterly in his power" (XV, p. 144).

Wooing Argemone and searching for a vocation, Lancelot is persuaded by Tregarva to investigate the condition of the agricultural laborers. To begin, Lancelot reads Blue Books and an unspecified book by Carlyle. Carlyle's book teaches him a truth not mentioned in the Blue Books: men have forgotten God. But the most direct lessons come through the gamekeeper himself. Tregarva tells Lancelot that the clergy are of little help to the laborers because the clergy fear the landlords on whose favor their living depends and because they seem to believe that men were made for the prayer-book, not the prayerbook for men. Further, though admitting the kindness of Honoria's charity, Tregarva deplores the fact that industrious men are dependent on alms. Shortly after, Tregarva is dismissed from service by Squire Lavington, who discovers the gamekeeper's incendiary poem against insensitive squires.

In the thematic center of the novel, a chapter ironically titled "The Village Revel," Tregarva takes Lancelot to a county fair. Here, Lancelot sees the legacy of the idle game-preserving aristocracy and of the Young England movement: hoping for a May-pole or for some other sign of pastoral joy, he finds only poverty and depravity.

By contrast with this chapter, the description of the foxhunt with which the novel begins apparently misrepresents the truth of the countryside. Yet each scene presents a view of reality; moreover, the contrast between them suggests a third view, one which reinforces Lancelot's lesson. Nature, as it appears in both chapters, is real: the countryside is beautiful, and those who labor in it are oppressed. The condition of the laborers, however, is caused not by nature, which is neutral, but by a privileged class that has forgotten its duties while enjoying its advantages.[7]

This exploitive relationship is paralleled by the affair between Colonel Bracebridge and Mary, a country girl whom he has ruined. The consequence of Bracebridge's seduction is that Mary kills their child and that Bracebridge, tormented by knowledge of the murder, commits suicide. The relationship of Bracebridge and Mary contrasts with that of Lancelot and Argemone. Love for Argemone ennobles Lancelot, and, as his love for her develops into love for all, he finds vocation in attempting to better the lot of the agricultural poor.

Shortly after returning from the village revel, Lancelot discovers that his fortune has been lost in the failure of his uncle's bank. In a conversation with his uncle, Lancelot disavows his lost wealth, declaring that he can no longer accept an income from a system he does not approve. He affirms his belief that biblical precepts are relevant to the laws of commerce and declares his faith in God's order of mutual love and trust.

Following close upon this conversation, Lancelot meets with his cousin Luke, who has recently converted to Catholicism. Also present is the smarmy priest who had persuaded Luke to convert. Luke represents for Kingsley the type of man who converts to Catholicism: "sincere but selfish, interested primarily in the salvation of his own soul, a little weak, not quite manly, in a word, un-English."[8] To Luke and the priest, Lancelot affirms his evolving faith: he seeks a living, masculine lord capable of ordering history and speaking to men. Fortuneless, Lancelot returns to Tregarva. The two men agree that the competitive system of manufacturing and shopkeeping is destroying the people. In order to effect a change, they decide to found a mission in an industrial town. But before they can do that, they need a leader. One appears in the mysterious prophet Barnakill.

Barnakill emphasizes the sanctity of nature, a doctrine toward which Lancelot has been working throughout the novel. Lancelot has already concluded that one comes to the beauty of the symbolized unseen through the beauty of the actual. Barnakill confirms Lancelot's conclusion by speaking to him of the possibility of finding the ideal in nature. Thus Barnakill suggests that Lancelot can be most fully Christian by being most fully a man. By accepting this idea, Lancelot takes a step toward what Kingsley's detractors would later call "muscular Christianity."

Shortly after this meeting, Lancelot is informed by Honoria that Argemone is dying of typhus contracted while ministering to the poor. Because of his loss of fortune and his increasingly radical attitudes, Lancelot had been rejected by the squire as a suitor for Argemone. Now Lancelot rushes to Argemone's bedside, where the two, who regard themselves as spiritually wed, reaffirm their love. She dies, willing Lancelot her fortune on the death of her mother. The novel closes as Barnakill arrives to take Tregarva and Lancelot to the utopian land of Prester John, described in medieval chronicles as a mythical kingdom of great beauty and justice located in the Far East and ruled by a king-priest lineally descended from the Magi who had visited the Christ-child. There they will learn of "Jesus Christ — THE MAN" (XV, p. 267). Once having learned their lesson, they will return to save England.

The basis for the story of Lancelot and Argemone is to be found in the lives of Charles and Fanny Kingsley. According to Fanny, Lancelot reflects Charles's early doubts and struggles. In addition,

Charles's biographers agree that the idea of "eye-wedlock" which appears in *Yeast* on the occasion of the lovers' first meeting, the initial dislike of Lancelot by Argemone's family, and the attitudes toward love and marriage conveyed by Lancelot are based on incidents and conversations in the lives of the Kingsleys themselves. One may also be tempted to find reflections of the actual Sir William Cope, Kingsley's patron at Eversley, in Squire Lavington, the idle aristocrat, and to hear Kingsley's difficulties with his patron echoed in Tregarva's remark that the clergy's fear of landlords contributes to England's problems. Likewise, as a country parson, Kingsley knew firsthand the poverty of the agricultural workers and the unhealthy effects of improper drainage.

Still, basing a novel on firsthand observation and personal experience does not guarantee its success. As a novel with a purpose, *Yeast* successfully presents Kingsley's case. It does so in part through its manipulation of character and plot. Both draw the earnest but unsettled Lancelot, conceived of as a characteristic young gentleman, to an acceptance of natural supernaturalism and a social mission based on biblical principles.

This singlemindedness produces flat rather than rounded characters, types instead of individuals, who are set off into contrasts that serve the message of the novel. Honoria and Argemone, for example, are opposites, both beautiful, but each lacking some quality the other has, the possession of which would form a single complete person. It is this division which the artist Claude Mellot senses when he wishes he were a Zeuxis who could unite them. Similarly, Lancelot and Tregarva are initially separated by class distinctions, but are finally spiritually united and given social purpose by the mysterious Barnakill. Barnakill, in effect, becomes the Zeuxis Claude Mellot is not; the result is a saving union not only of two men but also of the gentleman and the laborer they typify.

Singleness of purpose is also evident in Kingsley's plot. His handling of plot, however, is not so skillful as his handling of characterization nor is it as skillful in this his first novel as it would later become. The principal weakness in *Yeast* is that the novel is made of incidents which consist of opportunities for philosophical discussion but which never cohere. This weakness is most apparent as Kingsley tries to conclude. Barnakill, modeled on F. D. Maurice, has not appeared before but is acquainted with everyone except Lancelot. Near the end of the novel he appears unexpectedly at Lancelot's uncle's home, espousing a system of economics based upon Christian social morality, particularly the brotherhood of man, what Kingsley called "biblical economics"; he appears at the home of Claude and Sabina Mellot and discourses on the beauty of the actual as the revealer of ideal beauty; and he appears again at the end to remove Lancelot and Tregarva to the mysterious land of Prester John. In effect, the novel is not complete. The action simply stops as Lancelot, Tregarva, and Barnakill disappear toward a misty utopia.

Kingsley's method of handling characterization and plot, observable in *Yeast,* is also present in his later novels. Most of the themes developed in his first novel likewise remained his concerns for the rest of his life. His emphasis on the natural goodness of human affections sanctified by his belief that through them one understands the supernatural love of God, his belief that woman's true kingdom is of the heart and not of the head, his reveling in manliness and his consequent repudiation of Catholicism, and his indignation at the condition of the poor recur throughout his later novels. Thus, although Kingsley's art improved, his subjects remained fundamentally the same. From one point of view, *Yeast* presents the "essential" Kingsley.

III Alton Locke

Alton Locke, Tailor and Poet is one of several novels concerned with the "Condition of England Question" written during the 1840s and early 1850s. Disraeli's *Sybil; or, The Two Nations,* Elizabeth Gaskell's *Mary Barton* and *North and South,* Dickens's *Hard Times,* Frances Trollope's *Michael Armstrong, the Factory Boy,* sand Charlotte Brontë's *Shirley* are the most prominent. These authors, moved by their observations and stirred by their reading of social critics such as Thomas Carlyle and by their reading of Blue Book reports, enlisted fiction on the side of reform.

Alton Locke is the fictional autobiography of a young genius born into an impoverished Baptist working-class family in London. Just as *Yeast* deals with the problems of the agricultural poor, so *Alton Locke* is concerned with sweatshop conditions in the London tailors' trade, the failure of Chartism, and the effects of both on the development of the central character.

At an early age, Alton is put to work in a tailor's sweatshop. There he is introduced to radicalism by John Crossthwaite, a fellow tailor who denounces the clergy and the upper classes. Crossthwaite charges the clergy with keeping education from the people and declaims against the upper classes for assuring the poor of their concern while allowing them to die of preventable diseases. Fortunately, Alton comes under the moderating influence of the old radical Saunders Mackaye, a Scots bookseller modeled on Thomas Carlyle. Under Mackaye's guidance, Alton begins to educate himself.

After meeting and falling in love with Lillian, the daughter of Dean Winnstay, Alton realizes that his hopes for her are futile; his lack of opportunity has kept him down. But Mackaye, who has watched Alton's genius develop, tells him that if he wishes to get along among the well-to-do, he should write a book of poems. Nevertheless, he warns Alton that the danger of such an enterprise is that he may become a flunkey of the rich.

As Alton searches for a subject, Mackaye advises him to write about what he knows and takes him on a tour of London. Finding his topic to be the condition of the poor, Alton begins to write: "I had made up my mind, that if I had any poetic power, I must do my duty therewith in that station of life to which it had pleased God to call me, and to look at everything simply and faithfully as a London artisan" (VII, p. 208).

Two and a half years later, events coincide. Alton has written enough poems to fill a small octavo volume, and, under John Crossthwaite's influence, he declares himself a Chartist and loses his job. Taking Mackaye's advice, Alton goes to Cambridge to enlist the aid of his cousin George in finding a publisher. The walk from London to Cambridge gives Alton his first exposure to the countryside.

Amid the beauties of nature, Alton sees a gentleman fishing beside a stream. While he pauses to watch, there arrive a young, pretty yet simply dressed woman and a boy clad in Highland garb and riding on a pony. As the family gazes wonderingly at him, Alton, impressed by the differences between their condition and his, moves on. But he reflects that the incident is a paradigm of the relationship between the classes. He believes that in a "natural and harmonious state" society means brotherhood and that therefore one can receive aid from any stranger. For all he knows, the family might have offered him aid if they had known it was needed. By turning away, Alton feels he has maintained an artificial gulf between their class and his own. That he does not keep his promise to speak the truth of this insight through his poetry becomes a part of his tragedy.

At Cambridge, Alton becomes better acquainted with his cousin and is introduced to Lord Lynedale. As the days pass, Alton is disgusted by George, who has been influenced by Newman's sermons and who regards a career in the church as a guarantor of security. By contrast, Lord Lynedale rises in Alton's estimation. Although Alton initially dislikes Lord Lynedale for his apparent coldness, later acquaintance convinces him of Lynedale's "peculiar courtesy and liberality of mind toward those below him in rank" (VII, p. 264). Lord Lynedale, not George, offers to help Alton find a publisher. To this end he introduces Alton to Dean Winnstay.

During his visit in the Dean's home, Alton forms an immediate dislike for Eleanor Staunton, a follower of Carlyle. Alton's conversations with Eleanor range over a variety of topics. On religion and science, she suggests that Carlyle by holding the God of nature to be the God of man points the way toward the reconciliation of science and Christianity. On social conditions, she affirms her sympathy with the working classes, but emphasizes that the source of hostility between the workers and the clergy is the workers' lack of self-restraint. Genuine reform, she asserts, will occur only after the workers have reformed themselves and won the confidence of the clergy.

Eventually, the dean agrees to assist Alton in publishing his poems, but only if he will omit objectionable passages. These turn out to be the substance of the work, what Alton feels duty-bound to write. For the sake of publication, however, he agrees.

Alton returns to London, where he writes for the popular press, an occupation which forces him to choose continually between "the two great incompatibilities, what was true, and what would pay" (VIII, p. 38). Meanwhile, Eleanor marries Lord Lynedale, who comes into his inheritance and becomes Lord Ellerton; George wins a double-first at Cambridge and decides to seek ordination, despite his lack of preparation, and to marry Lillian.

The publication of Alton's poems brings Alton back into contact with the upper classes and elicits a warning from Mackaye not to allow himself to be destroyed by the wealthy and the well meaning. At the height of Alton's excitement, Lord Ellerton is killed in a fall from his horse and Fergus O'Flynn, editor of the Chartist *Weekly Warwhoop,* charges Alton in print with having deserted the People's Cause by compromising his poetry for the sake of sale. Each week brings a new attack, alienating Alton from the working class. At a Chartist meeting, however, Alton regains the respect of the workers when he volunteers to represent the London Chartists at a rally in the country.

On his second trip into the country, Alton sees what he had missed earlier; agricultural depression and the misery of the country poor. In scenes reminiscent of "The Village Revel" in *Yeast,* Alton describes the debilitating effects of the competitive system and political economy on agricultural laborers. At the rally, Alton addresses the crowd, which becomes uncontrollable and rushes off to pillage a nearby farm. By the time the riot has been put down, Alton, who had tried to stop it, is in jail awaiting trial. For his share in the event, he is sentenced to a three-year term. He is released just in time to participate in the presentation of the Charter.

Reflecting on the Charter, Alton believes it to be the product of the commercial class's betrayal of the workers after the passage of the Reform Bill of 1832. In 1832, the workers had supported the commercial class, but after the passage of the bill the commercial class had used its new powers to crush the workers. Alton remarks bitterly that the rebellion is not against law and the English constitution but against mammonism.

Alton and the other Chartists agree that the cause of their difficulties is competition among workers, which is the product of population growth and the prevailing Parliamentary belief in *laissez-faire* economics. The workers need relief, and Parliament claims to be powerless. The result is that the government does not design a comprehensive emigration scheme, prevent gluts in the labor market, or interfere between "slave and slave" or between "slave and tyrant" (VIII, p. 171).

As the presentation day nears, the workers' mood darkens, and fear of armed intervention pervades their ranks. Mackaye warns Alton and Crossthwaite that the petition is filled with bogus signatures. Old, and distressed by what he believes to be the workers' use of the devil's tools to do God's work, Mackaye dies. The debacle of April 10 passes as Mackaye had warned it would. Walking the streets in despair that evening, Alton chances upon Jemmy Downes, a former associate who is about to commit suicide. He returns Jemmy to his Jacob's Island home, a fetid chamber, the floor of which covers a sewer. On the floor are the bodies of Jemmy's family, partially eaten by rats and covered by the coats they had been sewing.

Although the deaths are clearly the result of disease, the police assume foul play. Their search for a murder weapon underlines for Alton the hypocrisy of law: careless to save people from tyranny, nakedness, and starvation, the law probes efficiently for "foul play," as if a knife were the only tool for murder. While the police search for a weapon, Jemmy leaps into a ditch behind his quarters and drowns.

Returning to his lodgings, Alton collapses. During his illness, he dreams of himself passing through stages of biological evolution until his fever breaks and he emerges from illness as if into a new life. Alton discovers that Mackaye has willed money to him and Crossthwaite on condition that they emigrate for seven years. Alton also learns that Eleanor has been working among needle-women in the East End and that she has organized a cooperative among them.

While Alton recuperates under Eleanor's and Crossthwaite's care, Eleanor teaches him that love is the living presence of God and that Christ is both the Great Reformer and the true conservative. The Bible, she says, is the only true Charter; and the Kingdom of God, she asserts, is founded on things better than acts of Parliament. Alton agrees that before one attempts to gain his rights, he must be sure he deserves them.

Alton inquires after Lillian. He is told that George has died and that Lillian has lost her beauty from the fever which felled Jemmy Downes's family. The coat which had covered the corpses of Jemmy's family had brought typhus to George and Lillian, thus proving the truth of Carlyle's lesson of the Irish widow in *Past and Present:* men are brothers regardless of their denial of relationship. Eleanor now tells her own story. Once vain, proud, intelligent, and dedicated to beauty, she was awakened by Lord Ellerton to the responsibilities of her station. She consequently became a philanthropist, seeking to serve God by serving Mammon and herself. She learned from Alton, however, that those below her might be more nearly her equals than she had suspected. Nevertheless, her attitude did not change until Lord Ellerton died. When institutions failed her, she turned to associations founded on faith, fraternal love, and the moral influence of Christianity. She learned to lead by example and thus she has attempted to show the nobility, who want to help, how to do it.

Alton is convinced that in order to effect the Kingdom of God in England, the workers need association, the aid of the clergy, and the good will and help of the upper classes. As he and Crossthwaite prepare for their seven years abroad, Alton learns that Eleanor's health is failing and that she will not accompany them. Alton and the Crossthwaite family set sail with the promise of a better future. Weeks later, off the coast of Texas, Crossthwaite enters Alton's cabin. He finds Alton dead, the ink still wet on the last entry — a poem — in his journal.

In *Alton Locke,* Kingsley's purpose is threefold: to discredit physical force Chartism, to particularize and assert the reality of the working man's problems in the face of the abstractions of political economy,[9] and to pose an alternative society based upon self-sacrifice and the brotherhood of man. In short, the novel proposes creating a society based upon Kingsley's conception of the Kingdom of God as an alternative to a society based upon competition and *laissez-faire* policies. In this novel, as in *Yeast* before, Kingsley subordinated the fictional devices of characterization, setting, and situation to the purpose which motivated his art: his wish to publicize and illustrate social evils which he felt to be of searing importance. In *Alton Locke,* he utilizes these devices with considerably more power than he had done in the earlier novel.

The major characters of *Alton Locke* serve as illustrations of either social problems or proposed solutions. Sandy Mackaye, a libertarian for sixty years, is a radical who knew the French Revolution. His age and wisdom persuade him that the proponents of the Charter are misdirected and bound to fail. John Crossthwaite exemplifies the class of decent working men driven by conditions and lack of self-restraint to approve violence as a means to gain Parliamentary acceptance of the Charter. Another type of "physical force" Chartist is the hack journalist Fergus O'Flynn. Modeled on Fergus O'Connor of the *Northern Star,* he exploits the People's cause for his own gain, stirring the masses to violence with half-truths and lies and then contriving to be out of town during the crisis of 1848. Mackaye, Crossthwaite, and O'Flynn represent three revolutionary types, with Mackaye clearly admired as the wisest.

Other characters which represent social attitudes are Lord Ellerton, Eleanor Staunton, Lillian, and George Locke. Lord Ellerton represents Young England, the active aristocrat seeking to reform his estates along paternalistic lines. His wife, Eleanor, as beautiful in spirit as she is in body, represents the concerned nobility, who, guided by Carlyle and the Mauricean conception of the Kingdom of God, is the best hope for genuine reform. On the other hand, Lillian is beautiful, but vain, selfish, and without compassion. She, therefore, must be punished by being made to lose her beauty through a disease caught because the fashions of her class are supplied by sweated labor. George Locke typifies Mammon, the ambitious, conscienceless middle class, and particularly that part of it which regards the Church as an institution to be used for guaranteeing social and financial security.

Each of these character types presents itself to the innocent Alton, who must choose from among them. As a working man, Alton has been denied education, the tool necessary for intelligent choice. He sets out, however, with the assistance of Mackaye to educate himself. The result is that before Alton finds the truth he is frequently beguiled and misled by those who would court but never wed him.

An author writing fiction of purpose constructs the elements of his work so that they will achieve his didactic goals. The risk he runs with characterization is that his inventions, functioning as spokesmen for moral and political points of view, will not become developed enough to transcend the limitations imposed by the author's purpose and will consequently fail to become thoroughly convincing or to remain so once the difficulties which prompted the work cease to exist. Implicit is a weakness in Kingsley's art: his characters are filled out in broad strokes to dramatize the social ills which aroused his moral indignation, but they are not finely shaded enough to be thoroughly convincing. Kingsley does better with setting. Descriptive prose is what Kingsley writes best, and in *Alton Locke* he skillfully manipulates the details of the setting to impress upon his reader correspondences between the physical and spiritual conditions of men. The most effective examples appear in the chapters "'The Yard Where the Gentlemen Live,'" "The Men Who Are Eaten," "The Lowest Deep," and "Dreamland."

The first two chapters mentioned present Alton's two journeys to the country. Here, setting joins with theme and character to portray the harsh realization that the Romantic vision of the countryside with its Wordsworthian beauty and Landseer-like idealization is on second glance as full of hardship as the sweater's den. On his first journey into the country, Alton is impressed by its beauty and by the picture-book scene played out by the curious gentleman and his family as they gaze at him in wonder from a background of stream, trees, and fence palings. Later he meets the yeoman Bob Porter, a Wordsworthian Michael whose son has been lost in the city. Alton's response to the first scene is embarrassment, indulgence in false pride, and a betrayal of both his class and the class of gentlemen willing to help but uncertain how best to do it. He then assists in rescuing Billy Porter from the sweater's den; "Michael's son" goes home and slips back into the romanticized countryside. On his second trip into the country, Alton faces the wretchedness of agricultural poverty and is jailed for his part in the sacking of a landowner's farm. It is as if Alton confronts a Michael, who, worn down by privation, ceases work on his sheepfold, joins with his neighbors, and runs riot in Grasmere Vale.

The last two chapters mentioned above are not companion pieces, as the two country journeys are. "The Lowest Deep" and "Dreamland," however, are noteworthy for their quality and for their concern with two subjects increasingly important for Kingsley: sanitation and biological evolution. In "The Lowest Deep," Kingsley describes living conditions in the Bermondsey district, which he had personally attempted to relieve only a few years before. The typhus-infested slum reaches out, infecting George and Lillian Locke through clothing made for them by sweated labor. In the "Dreamland" chapter, Alton, struggling to recover from typhus, dies a symbolic death to his previous life and dreams himself through successive stages of biological evolution into a new being. Under the spiritual care of Eleanor, Alton's moral and social views change, and, well enough to undertake his final journey, he gains faith in a Mauricean conception of the Kingdom of God.

Complementing this presentation of physical setting and situation is Kingsley's portrayal of Alton's early spiritual environment. Under the influence of his dissenting mother and her Calvinist friends, Alton lives his early life deprived even of the hope promised by belief in a personal, loving God. Alton sees himself as the victim of a theology which tolerates poverty by postponing redress for suffering to the next life and which deprives the poor even of imaginative pleasure by denying them art and literature. Thus, the dissenters aggravate the condition of the poor instead of alleviating it. The Church of England is little better. Coming from the upper classes, its parsons at best often do not understand the despair of the poor and at worst are frequently derelict at their duties; or they are, like George, interested only in using the church as a means of self-aggrandisement.

In this physical and spiritual environment, Kingsley portrays the growth of atheism and violence among the working classes. Deprived and exploited by their betters, the working classes resort in despair to violence and thereby unwittingly fall victim to the unscrupulous among themselves and ironically seem to confirm the opinion held of them by the upper classes.

Although sympathizing with the working classes, Kingsley believed that physical force was not an effective device for obtaining justice. *Alton Locke* is an attempt to discredit physical force Chartism by portraying it as ineffective. It is ineffective, Kingsley implies, because it ignores the spiritual condition of men, divides the classes through demagoguery, and serves only to arouse the opposition's force. The ineffectiveness of physical force is made clear in the country riot, which sends Alton to jail, and in the ill-fated attempt to present the 1848 Charter. Ignoring the workers' innate desire for justice, the advocates of physical force appeal only to lower instincts. The result is that a display of righteous anger at a meeting in the country is turned by demagoguery into a riot which is broken up by the constabulary. In the city, the Chartist demonstration aroused by the likes of Fergus O'Flynn collapses in the presence of a specially organized police force and the humiliation which follows when many signatures on the petition are revealed to have been forged. In both instances, the workers are set into opposition against the upper classes, who respond with force. Kingsley's point is that movements which divide classes are socially destructive.

With this lesson in mind, Kingsley points out a constructive alternative to physical force Chartism. Through the growth of the central character, Kingsley portrays the making of a physical force Chartist and his subsequent remaking along Christian lines.[10] After his symbolic death and rebirth, Alton is taught by Eleanor that social and political beliefs cannot be isolated from their religious roots. This is so because man can gain "freedom" only through the activation of his whole being, and such activation can occur only through the liberating power of Jesus. As long as Alton seeks "freedom" through Chartism, a movement which has lost sight of spiritual ends, he founders.[11] Thus, in Kingsley's view, only on the Christian principles of cooperation and self-sacrifice can men ground society with hope of prosperity and permanence.[12]

In spite of their egalitarian appearance, however, Kingsley's social attitudes are predominantly paternalistic. In his cooperative scheme, it is clear who should lead and who should follow. It is

Eleanor, the awakened member of the upper classes, who becomes the spokesman for the coming social order. Kingsley believes that the workers should have better surroundings and better opportunities for education, but the life of Alton Locke should also teach the ambitious worker to know his class and to stay within it, helping it to rise, as a class, to the best that is in it.[13] By choosing to leave the path God intends for him, Alton forfeits a happiness within his reach. For Kingsley, then, Alton's fall is not caused by the circumstances of his life but by his own unwise choice.[14]

IV Two Years Ago

Between the publication of *Alton Locke* in 1850 and *Two Years Ago* in 1857, Kingsley published two historical novels, *Hypatia* and *Westward Ho!* In *Two Years Ago,* Kingsley returned to the contemporary scene, focusing on the Crimean War, the issues of sanitation and public health, and slavery in the United States. In its direct representation of contemporary affairs, and particularly in its treatment of the problems of sanitation and public health, *Two Years Ago* is thematically more closely linked to *Yeast* and *Alton Locke* than to Kingsley's historical novels.

Two Years Ago begins in the present with a chapter titled "Introductory." In it Stangrave, an American and a political Fremonter; Claude Mellot, an artist familiar to us from *Yeast;* and Mark Armsworth, a banker, are situated in the countryside and are discussing improvements in the quality of life since 1848. Since the introduction of free trade and the beginning of emigration, the laborers admit to being better off than they have been for fifty years. The three companions note various agricultural reforms and agree that it is "hopeful" to see the aristocracy bringing taste and knowledge to bear on the lower classes. Everywhere they look, they see improvements: Lord Minchampstead has established schools and a library for farm laborers, the local miller's daughter is reading Charlotte Yonge's novels and teaching in a National School, and Lord Vieuxbois, who had fought bravely in the Crimea, is lecturing in the Mechanic's Institutes.

Then, in a lengthy flashback, Kingsley picks up his story at its beginning, sixteen years earlier. Two young men, Tom Thurnall and John Briggs, live with Tom's father, a doctor. Tom is full of high spirits and intelligence, loves jokes and adventure, and, in spite of his apparent nonchalance, is cool and efficient in his work. Briggs,

however, is Byronic: he affects black curly hair and a turned-down
collar. He is melancholy and ambitious; regarding himself as a
"pegasus in harness," he believes he could accomplish great things
if only he had more scope.

Dr. Thurnall advises Briggs as Sandy Mackaye had advised
Alton: work where God has placed you. But Briggs has been
reading Percy's *Reliques* and the life of Chatterton and conceives
himself to be a priest of beauty. He is, however, less concerned with
beauty than with his own sensations. Briggs goes to London, where
he changes his name to Elsley Vavasour, publishes *The Soul's
Agonies and Other Poems,* and thereby becomes a seriocomic version of the spasmodic poet.

Tom also leaves home. The autumn of 1853 finds him working
Australian gold fields. While there Tom is informed of his
brother's death and his father's approaching blindness and financial ruin. He sails for home with £1,500 in a moneybelt. As Tom
nears the English coastal town of Aberalva, Kingsley introduces
Grace Harvey, a beautiful dissenter and schoolmistress; Frank
Headley, the village's High-Church curate; and a number of local
residents. Also dwelling nearby are the unhappy occupants of
Penalva Court, Mr. and Mrs. Elsley Vavasour. Mrs. Vavasour is
the former Lucia St. Just, sister of Lord Scoutbush.

When Tom's ship sinks in a storm off the coast, he is rescued by
Grace and a group of local sailors. Recovering in the home of Dr.
Heale, an incompetent physician whose practice he eventually takes
over, Tom misses his moneybelt. Concluding that one of his res-
cuers has stolen it, he suspects Grace because she had placed her
arms around him as he was dragged ashore. Tom decides to remain
in Aberalva and recover his money.

Tom hears from an American quadroon whom he had freed
from slavery several years before that she has taken the name Maria
Cordifiamma, become an actress, and set sail for London. She arrives at the home of Claude and Sabina Mellot followed by Stangrave, a would-be suitor. Once in England, Maria is adored by the
titled and the wealthy. But Maria refuses to marry anyone who
does not devote his life to a cause.

Settled into his medical practice and his scientific studies, Tom
comes upon Elsley at the seashore. Tom is gathering specimens;
Elsley is trying to write poetry. Because of his self-absorption,
Elsley's poetic well is drying up. He has shut himself off from reality, forgotten the virtues of gentleness and home, and allowed his

marriage to deteriorate. Consequently, his poems have become more concerned with sensuous beauty than with moral tone, and manner has begun to replace matter. As Elsley tries to versify, Tom reveals to him under a microscope beauty which his sensation-seeking has caused him to miss. Because Tom, the naturalist, is grounded in reality, he is more alert to beauty than is John Briggs, the poet.

While these events transpire, Frank Headley's attempt to win his parish from chapel to church continues without success. Having become friends with Tom, Frank discusses with him the substance of his sermons and the celibacy of the clergy. Tom tells Frank that the simple, natural things are also the divine things and that the idea of the celibacy of the clergy is a diabolical dodge for preventing parsons from understanding humanity. Tom concludes that Frank will be a good parson if he will find a wife.

As if in response to Tom's suggestion, Valentia St. Just, the flirtatious sister of Lord Scoutbush and Lucia Vavasour, enters the story. Frank is immediately smitten and then falls into confusion: he had intended to remain celibate; he now tries to convince himself that Valentia will make a good wife. She is above him in station, however, and therefore apparently out of reach. Although attracted to Frank's air of "true melancholy," Valentia flirts with Elsley, flattering his ego and unwittingly hastening the deterioration of her sister's home.

By June 1854, the lives of the principal characters seem complicated beyond repair. Adding to the difficulties, Tom realizes that cholera will soon break out. But the residents of Aberalva, seeing no relationship between crowding and cholera and unimpressed by Tom's evidence, refuse to prepare. The people also oppose Tom because for them to agree with him would be to admit to having lived unclean lives for generations and to having to accept responsibility for their illnesses and those of their children.

Anxiously trying to save the people from the consequences of their ignorance and obstinacy, Tom asks Frank to preach on the subject of sanitation, a topic Kingsley himself had broached numerous times. When Frank objects to preaching on a "secular" topic, Tom argues that preaching about sanitation falls under the commandment "Thou shalt not kill." Convinced, Frank preaches on the subject and is denounced by the dissenters. Tom turns to Elsley, to Lord Scoutbush, and finally to the national government. Elsley and Scoutbush do nothing, the one from cowardice and the other from conclusions based on false information supplied by his overseer. The government promises to send an inspector, but only after cholera has broken out. Becoming desperate, Tom attempts to enlist Grace's influence with the people. Grace explains to Tom the dissenters' belief that sanitary reform is unacceptable because it interferes with the judgment of God. Tom counters this argument by asserting that preventable diseases are God's judgment against filth and ignorance. Grace assists Tom's cause.

When the disease appears, Tom is assisted by Frank, Lord Scoutbush, Grace, and Major Campbell, a naturalist hopelessly in love with Lucia Vavasour. The cholera fighters must battle not only the disease but also sectarian theology. Sectarians preaching that cholera is the judgment of God and using fear of disease to frighten people into fear of hell are eventually silenced at a revival meeting. There, Major Campbell takes over. He appeals to "manhood" and to married women, leaving the revivalist sputtering to "hussies," who enjoy falling into fits. Typically for Kingsley, the men are struck by Campbell's matter, the wives by his manner. Calling upon God to choose between him and the revivalist, Campbell sees that judgment made as the revivalist collapses and dies from cholera.

During the epidemic, Frank declares his love to Valentia, who acknowledges her need for male leadership. As Frank's earnest simplicity increases through his love for Valentia, his preaching improves. Thus, as the epidemic passes, Frank begins to win the people his High-Church attitudes had lost. Even Grace is converted to Broad Church Anglicanism.

While Frank and Valentia's love grows, Elsley and Lucia's withers. Tormented by jealousy of Major Campbell, Elsley deserts his family and goes to London, where he becomes addicted to laudanum. Major Campbell follows but cannot overtake Elsley. In London, Campbell meets Tom, who is on his way to the Crimea. The major and Tom locate Elsley, whom Tom persuades to return to his childhood home. On his deathbed, Elsley reveals to Lucia his real name and asks her to burn his poetry. After Elsley's death, Tom, Major Campbell, Frank, and Lord Scoutbush go to the Crimea, but not before Tom has seen Stangrave, who has taken Maria's abolitionist cause as his own and thereby won her.

With Tom in the Crimea, Grace's mother admits to having stolen his moneybelt. Determined to return the money to Tom and prove her innocence, Grace goes to the Crimea to find him. She nurses at

Scutari and Balaklava, but is unable to locate Tom. At the war's end, she obtains a position in the home of Tom's father and waits.

One by one the veterans return, all but Campbell, who dies, and Tom, who has been taken prisoner. When Tom finally returns, Grace hands him the moneybelt. At first, she does not recognize that he is a chastened man. As they take each other in their arms, Tom admits that for the first time in his life he has known fear. In the Russian prison, he has found that he needs God. As the novel ends, the "muscular" Tom is ready to be Christianized.

Like all of Kingsley's fiction, *Two Years Ago* is topical and didactic. For modern readers, one of its principal attractions is that it still manages to convey Kingsley's sense of urgency concerning the mid-Victorian issues of sanitation, the American abolitionist movement, and the Crimean War. Between the writing of *Alton Locke* and *Two Years Ago,* Kingsley had published two historical novels, *Hypatia* and *Westward Ho!* In the movement of its characters throughout the world and in the plot and subplot, *Two Years Ago* exhibits the length and scope of the two intervening works. In its flashes of satirical wit, however, the novel looks back to Fergus O'Flynn and the *Weekly Warhoop* in *Alton Locke* and forward to *The Water-Babies.*

In *Two Years Ago,* Kingsley wished to demonstrate his belief that to be successful men must be physically and morally strong and must submit their strength to the guidance of God. The main plot illustrates this point through the development of Tom Thurnall from arrogant self-assurance to recognition of his dependence on God.[15] According to Kingsley's scheme, the ideal protagonist is "manly"; that is, he is physically vital and, recognizing in his vitality and natural drives the goodness of God, he willingly submits his vitality to divine guidance. Such a man is a "muscular Christian." He is earnest. He marries and sires children. He fights cholera, social injustice, or the Russians, and he builds empires.

This ideal protagonist is that character type toward which the novel moves. Tom's character is determined by that purpose; the problem is that he is unconvincing. Tom is supposed to embody muscularity eventually tempered by recognition of the need for divine guidance. Throughout the novel, however, he is portrayed as a shrewd, cunning, and selfish man who uses his medical skill as a device to gain power over the residents of Aberalva and to advance himself.[16] Kingsley's portrayal of Tom's end-of-the-novel conversion does not ameliorate 400 pages of swagger and bravado.

Kingsley's point concerning "manliness" is reinforced by his treatment of the relative successes and failures of three characters who serve as foils to Tom. At the opposite pole from Tom is Elsley Vavasour, who cultivates neither manliness nor love of the natural world and thereby isolates himself from God, from the love of his wife, and from the wellspring of poetry. The result is that he becomes enamored of his own sensations, seeks escape from his problems in laudanum, and dies pitiably. As a clergyman, Frank Headley is aware of man's need for divine guidance, but his High-Church views are no more grounded in reality than is Elsley's poetry. By holding such views, Frank unintentionally alienates his simple parishioners, and frustrates his genuine wish to be of service. Through love for Valentia and through his ministry during the Aberalva cholera epidemic, Frank discovers the sanctity of the natural affections and the moral influence of the English home. Abandoning his High-Church ways and growing in manliness, he succeeds as a priest. Unlike Elsley and Frank, Major Campbell is already a muscular Christian. The major is a biologist whose love of nature has led him to love of God; he is therefore firmly grounded in reality. Like Tom, Elsley, and Frank, however, Major Campbell can be judged by his response to the inspirational love for a woman. Tom's eventual peace of mind is promised at the end of the novel when he takes Grace in his arms and seeks to learn of God through her. Elsley's peace is destroyed by his willful isolation from the love of his wife. Frank is raised into true manliness by his love for Valentia and succeeds as a clergyman through the influence of her homely affection. Early in his career, Major Campbell fell in love with Lucia, who, unaware of the major's feelings, married Elsley. The major was therefore isolated from the happiness of marriage, but was nevertheless inspired by his secret devotion to perform soldierly and merciful acts, doing his duty in Aberalva and in the Crimea.

In the subplot, a similar set of circumstances exists, except there they are tied to the question of slavery in the United States. The American, Stangrave, pursues Maria Cordifiamma across Europe, winning her only after promising to espouse her cause. Through his love of Maria and through his dedication of himself to her cause, the life of Stangrave, an accomplished but unproductive man, is given purpose. The principal difficulty with the subplot is that it is intrusive, allowing Kingsley to comment on American problems, but making the structure of the novel "higgledy-piggledy."[17]

The purpose of the novel, then, determines its plot structure by setting up its male characters in relation to each other so as to illustrate their moral success or failure. Furthermore, their chance for success is dependent upon their acceptance of nature and their "natural" affections, their instincts, as good and upon their recognition of the interdependence of physical strength and divine guidance as the basis of heroism. Kingsley's female characters support the men they love, for only so are the deepest needs of their womanly nature satisfied. Through love, men and women attain a completeness otherwise unattainable.

The most important female characters in the main plot are Grace Harvey and the sisters Lucia Vavasour and Valentia St. Just. Maria Cordifiamma, the quadroon actress and former slave, appears in the subplot. Grace Harvey is a schoolteacher and a member of the Brianite Chapel, not the Church of England. Her nearly mystical sensibilities allied to her devotion to God and the children of Aberalva have made her beloved by the rough citizen-sailors of the town. Grace's dissenting views conflict with the High-Church views of Frank Headley, who initially seeks to replace her as teacher. Her love for Tom Thurnall, however, combines with their metaphysical discussions and her experience during the cholera epidemic to reveal to her the narrowness of her sectarian beliefs. She and Frank approach an acceptable Broad Church position from opposite poles, she from the Brianite Chapel and he from the airy influence of Oxford.

By the end of the novel, Grace has become acceptably Broad Church and has settled in old Dr. Thurnall's home to await Tom's return. When Tom appears, drawn to his father by the love that has steadied him throughout his life, he is a chastened man. But if love of his father has sustained him thus far in his life, love of Grace will assure him of the goodness of God and provide a direction for his manhood lacking heretofore. Grace cannot live fully without Tom, nor can he realize his potential without her. Through the influence of earthly and natural love, which mirrors and is sanctified by the love of God, Tom is redeemed by Grace.

The two other women in the main plot are the sisters Lucia and Valentia. Because Kingsley intends them to dramatize forms of moral action, they instinctively desire to be led by manly strength, and their lives are either heavenly or hellish in direct proportion to the manliness of their respective husbands. Lucia falls in love with

Elsley's Byronic curls. Always enamored more of his own sensations than of the beauties of the real world, Elsley loses the abiding pleasure and steadying influence of love and is driven mad by his own impulses. Elsley ignores Lucia, whose love is frustrated and whose life is made wretched by her husband's petty jealousies and effeminacy. One of their children dies, Elsley dies, and finally Lucia dies, broken and unhappy.

Valentia is more fortunate. Her beauty, charm, and wit awaken manliness in Frank. Unlike Grace and Lucia, Valentia masks ennui with a frivolous pose. She finds in Frank as he ministers to cholera patients and as he himself recovers from the disease, an earnestness she has never known. As her beauty awakens Frank to the possibilities of love, his earnestness awakens Valentia to her innate desire to submit her weakness to his strength. Through love of her, Frank realizes his manliness and becomes a successful priest. Through love of him, Valentia fully realizes her femininity and becomes the ideal biblical helpmate.

In the subplot, Maria Cordifiamma passes herself off as an Italian actress and comes to England pursued by her would-be suitor Stangrave. She ignites aristocratic hearts with love, but maintains a melodramatic hauteur that keeps her admirers at a distance. Maria, however, has the sexual drives of other Kingsley women and secretly wishes to marry a hero who will espouse her cause as well as herself. But Maria's misery has another cause as well, one which Kingsley hints at but the consequence of which he avoids. Maria is a quadroon, neither black nor white, whose struggle to come to terms with her own identity is potentially, for a modern reader, at least, the most interesting part of the story. In a crucial scene early in the novel, she replies to Stangrave's impassioned pleas that a "great gulf" lies between them. Seated before a mirror, she is transfixed by her reflection, not from vanity, but from disgust. Her imagination causes her to look for signs of African features and, as she looks, she makes a face that appears African. As Stangrave shudders at the sight, Maria recalls the memory of an ancient Negress called granny by her mother. Confused, Stangrave leaves her when she cries out to him to let her bear her curse alone.

Melodrama takes over. Stangrave eventually learns the truth about Maria and becomes a Fremonter, advocating free soil and free men in territories to which slavery had not spread, and therefore heroic enough to justify Maria's marrying him. Stangrave's conversion from idle dilettantism to work as a Fremonter and his marriage to Maria, moderating her more radical abolitionist position, support the novel's theme of and Kingsley's belief in the redemptive character of work and resolve the romantic problem of the subplot. But this leaves unresolved the question of Maria's divided self, and it keeps at a secure distance the enslaved blacks on whose behalf Maria labors. Through the character of the racially troubled Maria, Kingsley appears at first to favor abolition; however, by marrying her to Stangrave, he shows that he does not.[18] Instead, he advocates preventing the spread of slavery to newly opening territories and allowing it to die out through attrition in the slave states.

Relief from the weight of Kingsley's major themes is provided occasionally by his satirical wit, which leavens the novel's earnest dough. For example, names animate Kingsley's sense of fun. In the Australian goldfields, Tom meets an Englishman from "Nomansland-cum-Clayhole." Back in England, he meets an undisciplined and drunken squireen named Trebooze, who lives at "Liberty Hall." "Hatchgoose" is the publisher of a literary magazine with which Vavasour is associated. Hatchgoose sponsors a "Mutual Puffery Society" for his male and female authors. A few other examples will suffice: The Rev. Dionysius O'Blareaway, a popular Irish preacher from the West End; Lady Knockdown, the Irish aunt of Lord Scoutbush; Hector Harkaway, an Irish novelist; and Baron Torytown, whose politics are self-evident.

Most of the satire, however, is directed at Elsley and his literary circle. Two scenes are especially notable. The first occurs early in the novel. In the office of Dr. Heale, Tom and Elsley discuss Elsley's poetry. Elsley believes that Tom has not recognized him. Tom has read Elsley's volume *The Soul's Agonies,* which he says he has lost. He does not mention that he "lost" it by pitching it into the Colorado River. Elsley offers to send Tom a copy of a later volume, telling him that he is sure to find it an improvement. Tom replies, "How can I doubt that I shall?" (XIII, p. 137). Elsley leaves the shop, and Tom, overcome by Elsley's absurdity, performs an Indian war dance, which calls to mind the antics of Jim Dixon in Kingsley Amis's novel *Lucky Jim.*

Later, in a description of a meeting of Hatchgoose's Mutual Puffery Society, Kingsley satirizes the literary set which formed round the periodicals of the time. Once again, Elsley is included. He has been a writer and subeditor for various magazines and is

thus a member of the Society. As a poet, he is bound by "honour
and green tea." The description of the literary world represented,
its meannesses and the hope for the favor of the great, is reminiscent of that world which attracted Alton Locke. Here, however,
the presentation has a satirical edge missing in the earlier book,
where its presentation had to appear alluring enough to convince
readers that Alton's fall is understandable. The self-conscious
literary society in *Two Years Ago* is presented as grotesque and
unappealing. Among the members are women authors who have
quarreled with their husbands and therefore have become advocates of women's rights, or unmarried women who have formu-
lated model schemes of education for children they have never had.
In this scene, Kingsley makes clear that only neurotic self-servers
such as Elsley seek membership.

CHAPTER 4

An Evolutionary Fantasy:
The Water Babies

IN the 1830s religious doubt came from Germany to England
through the works of Gotthold Lessing and Johann Gottfried
von Herder, who had inspired a study of the grammar and
philology of the Bible. These "lower critics" assumed the Bible to
be a human product which exhibited the sort of textual difficulties
found in other ancient texts. On the basis of their studies, the
"lower critics" announced that Moses did not write the Pentateuch, that the traditional attributes of authorship could not be
trusted, and that the books of the Bible had undergone frequent
editorial revisions.

If the texts of the Bible were inaccurate, could one trust their
contents? Following the suggestions of Immanuel Kant and the
post-Kantian idealists Johann Gottlieb Fichte, Friedrich von
Schelling, and Georg Wilhelm Friedrich Hegel, a number of critics
proposed that although the Bible may be inaccurate as an historical
record, it presents a higher kind of truth.[1]

The first of the "higher critics" to be known in Germany was
David Strauss, whose *Das Leben Jesu* (1835) appeared in a complete English version translated by Mary Ann Evans (later famous
as George Eliot) in 1846 as *The Life of Jesus*. Like the "lower
critics," Strauss examined the Bible and found an absence of literal
truth. Unlike them, he declared that the absence of literal truth did
not matter, for the Gospels are myths. Hegel had taught Strauss
that religion is "the perception of truth . . . invested with
imagery."[2] Consequently, Strauss asserted, factual errors and con-
tradictions in the Gospels are to be expected. The truth of the myth
is independent of particular errors and confusions. In fact, according to Strauss, one must come to see the facts as trivial in order
to see the central message of Christianity. For Strauss, the central

67

message of the Gospels was that the Absolute is Humanity and that Jesus' significance lies in his having taught the proper attitude toward Humanity. Humanity became, for Strauss, the Christ which unites the human and spiritual natures and thus which permits "the individual man [to] participate in the divinely human life of the species."[3]

Other "higher critics" offered other interpretations, none of which proved congenial to literal-minded Englishmen, and in the 1860s the textual attacks continued. In 1860, seven English authors presented without criticism some of the results of recent German studies. The publication of their *Essays and Reviews* struck many Victorians as an attempt to destroy Christianity. Following a series of trials and hearings, a group of 11,000 clergymen signed a petition asserting their conviction that belief in the everlasting torment of the damned and the literal truth of the Bible were necessary dogmas of their church. In 1862, John Colenso, Bishop of Natal, employed his mathematical training in studying the Pentateuch and located so many self-contradictions that he concluded its narrative cannot be historically accurate. Colenso's argument followed the Broad Church position that the Bible is not the essence of religion, for God reveals himself not only in the Bible but also in the hearts of men.

Religious doubt raised by the analysis of biblical texts was shattering enough, but when scientific studies attacked religious certainty from another direction, Victorians were doubly unsettled. In the 1840s the implications for religion of scientific studies began to be clear. The discoveries of geologists appeared to support the contentions of the "lower" and "higher" critics of the Bible by calling into question the trustworthiness of the literal historical truth of the Bible; for example, the age of the earth appeared much greater than the Mosaic account indicated. More serious was the growing agreement among geologists that "the configuration of the earth's surface could not be explained by catastrophes . . . and must be explained by uniform causes working slowly through immense stretches of time."[4]

Toward the end of the eighteenth century, William Paley had given the argument from design its most popular exposition. The argument from design is very old, and, in its barest form, very simple: the innumerable parts of our complex universe appear to have been arranged by an intelligent creator with a rational purpose; the simplest explanation of this observation is that an intelligent creator exists and that he has a rational purpose. Paley's exposition was widely current during the nineteenth century in both his texts and those of later commentators on them.

For the Victorians, the principal difficulty with the argument from design was that it treated "the existence and attributes of God as a sort of scientific hypothesis which explains the facts of the universe."[5] Geological and biological studies during the nineteenth century increasingly suggested that other hypotheses provided better explanations. In 1830 Charles Lyell published his *Principles of Geology,* arguing that uniform and unchanging laws had been and were still transforming the surface of the earth and that therefore the age of the earth had to be reckoned in the millions of years. In 1844 Robert Chambers published anonymously his *Vestiges of Creation,* proposing an hypothesis which accounts for the appearance of design in the universe without reliance on the presence of a designer. By 1844, then, these popular geological studies had suggested that the earth is considerably older than biblical chronology allows and that the appearance of design in the universe can be accounted for without supposing the existence of God.

In 1859 Charles Darwin's *Origin of Species by Means of Natural Selection* placed before a religiously troubled audience not only a mass of evidence cautiously and unpolemically explained but also the hypothesis that the struggle for existence determines animal evolution. Darwin had suggested that what appeared in nature to be the product of design could be the result of chance. In 1871 Darwin fulfilled the fears of many by presenting in *The Descent of Man* his conclusion that scientific methods could be applied to the study of man.

One scientific study after another seemed to demonstrate that the universe is governed by laws. As they did, fundamental questions arose concerning the possibility of God's providential interruption and direct guidance of his creation, of the possibility of free will, and of the efficacy of prayer. "It began to seem to many religious believers that the only room left for their beliefs was the holes as yet uncovered by scientific knowledge. And Science . . . was continuously closing gaps."[6] At the heart of the Victorians' difficulty is their belief that the controversy between science and religion is a controversy over the nature and limits of knowledge. The Victorians' philosophical inheritance was dominated by empiricism, the central principle of which is that knowledge is limited to what we can experience through our senses and infer from our exper-

ience. If science was not destroying religion, it was causing it to retreat into regions which had little or no bearing on either the
meaning or the conduct of life.

Throughout his career, Kingsley was fascinated by the study of
natural science. His prose idylls and his novels are packed with
details drawn from moorland and fen or from descriptions of
exotic vegetation. In each case, Kingsley imbues close observation
of nature with moral purpose, keeping such observation within a
Christian context and implicitly sustaining his belief that genuine
art is firmly grounded in the actual. Kingsley's standing as a naturalist is indicated by his acquaintance with the biologist Philip
Gosse, to whom he sent specimens, and by his friendship with the
scientists Charles Bunbury and Charles Lyell, both of whom nom-
inated him in 1863 as a Fellow of the Geological Society. In 1854,
Kingsley had written "The Wonders of the Shore" for the *North
British Review*. In 1855, he had published an expanded version,
Glaucus; Or, The Wonders of the Shore, as a volume. *Glaucus* encourages holiday-makers at the seaside to do what Kingsley himself
habitually did: turn idleness to profit by examining seaside marine
life. The reward for such holiday labor, Kingsley advised, would be
the discovery of greater wonders than even opium eaters have
dreamed. Evident in the book is Kingsley's acceptance of evolutionary processes which have been at work over countless ages to
produce the world we know.

Kingsley's fascination with natural science was lifelong. So was
his interest in children. In 1856, he had written *The Heroes,* a retelling of the stories of Perseus, the Argonauts, and Theseus. In
1868, Kingsley wrote "Madam How and Lady Why" for the
journal *Good Words for the Young,* publishing it in volume form
in 1870 as *Madam How and Lady Why; Or, First Lessons in Earth
Lore for Children.* The underlying principle of Kingsley's lessons is
that one should learn what his senses can teach in order to understand better their limitations. Kingsley emphasizes that the most
glorious and true things are not material and therefore are not open
to the senses. The point of *Madam How and Lady Why* is a varia-
tion on the theme of *Glaucus:* close observation of the natural
world prepares one for life by rooting him firmly in the actual and
by pointing to an immaterial glory indicated but not defined by the
study of physical reality.

In *The Water-Babies,* first published in *Macmillan's Magazine* in
1862 and issued as a volume in 1863, Kingsley placed the nine-

teenth-century conflict between science and religion in the context of a fantasy designed to reconcile them by showing continuous development to be the creative principle at work in the world. Through the death, moral growth, and eventual rebirth of the central character, Kingsley links the principles of evolution in the physical world to the growth and maturity of the spiritual being, reaffirming the message in the earlier *Glaucus* and pointing toward it in the later *Madam How and Lady Why*. Victorian children, taught by Kingsley's fantasy, should see that an imaginative vision of the material world opens to them a spiritual reality not perceptible by the senses alone. These children should be able to accept the advance of science without losing their Christian faith.

I The Water-Babies

At Harthover Place, a grand country house with many game preserves, Tom and his master, Grimes, prepare to sweep the chimneys. A mistreated apprentice and a city boy, Tom is used to neither the country nor the grandeur of Harthover Place. When he becomes lost in the chimneys and descends into the snow-white bedchamber of the squire's daughter Ellie, Tom recognizes for the first time in his life that he is dirty. He is suddenly ashamed and angry.

Frightened when the child awakens, Tom climbs out a window and runs away through the woods. Nearly exhausted, he comes to a hilltop and looks down into a valley where a schoolteacher tends her garden and a clear stream flows near a schoolhouse. Churchbells seem to be ringing in the valley as Tom descends, followed at a distance by a mysterious Irishwoman.

In the valley, Tom falls ill. The schoolteacher feeds him and puts him to bed in a building near the school. In his fevered dream, Tom continues to hear the sound of churchbells, and, conscious of being dirty, he believes he hears the schoolteacher and the Irishwoman suggesting that he wash. Repeating to himself, "I must be clean," Tom walks to the stream. Looking into the water, he sees the Irishwoman, who has disrobed and joined the fairies of the stream. Later, finding Tom's body, the squire and his men mistakenly believe the boy to have drowned. Tom, however, has not died. He has merely shed his earthly husk and been transformed by the fairies into a water-baby. In his new form, Tom forgets his previous existence and, like a child on holiday, revels in the underwater kingdom.

When a storm arises, many of the creatures of the stream begin swimming to the ocean. Tom observes that the salmon, the most gentlemanly fish, are eager to reach the sea. Joining them, he watches a battle between keepers and poachers and recognizes Grimes as one of the poachers. Tom becomes apprehensive when he sees Grimes fall into the stream and drown; he fears that the fairies will transform Grimes into a water-baby and that he will be troublesome again. Tom, however, swims to the sea, where he feels happy.

Meanwhile, Ellie is walking along the shore with Professor Ptthmllnsprts and arguing about the existence of water-babies. During the course of the debate, they catch Tom, who manages to slip away and return to the water. Ellie falls into the sea and drowns, whereupon she is given wings by the fairies.

Shortly after his escape from the professor, Tom, at great peril, frees a lobster friend from a pot. After performing this altruistic act, Tom discovers that other water-babies had been around him all along, but he had been unable to recognize them. From his new acquaintances, Tom learns that the home of the water-babies is St. Brandon's Isle, the place known to Plato as Atlantis. When he arrives there, Tom finds thousands of water-babies; they are children who have been mistreated or who have died of preventable diseases.

Tom misbehaves and is reprimanded by Mrs. Bedonebyasyoudid. On Sunday Mrs. Doasyouwouldbedoneby arrives. She is the sister of Mrs. Bedonebyasyoudid, and she pays special attention to Tom, cuddling him and singing to him as his mother had never done. Being comfortable, however, makes Tom misbehave again. He breaks into Mrs. Doasyouwouldbedoneby's candy chest and eats what he believes to be all of the candy. Tom's naughtiness creates prickles on his body.

When Tom confesses and wishes to be rid of his prickles, the fairies assign Ellie to teach him how to be good. Tom is told that he can go to the beautiful place where Ellie dwells only after he has located and assisted Mr. Grimes. But Tom is afraid, and fear makes him petulant. The fairies believe that Tom has been in the nursery long enough and that he must aid Grimes alone. Consequently, Mrs. Bedonebyasyoudid tells Tom the story of the Doasyoulikes, a self-indulgent group who, because they avoided work, suffered reverse evolution: beginning as men, they ended as apes, becoming extinct when the last of them was shot by a hunter.

In order to find Grimes, Tom must seek directions from Mother Carey, a mysterious woman, whose home Tom locates only after a long search, which culminates in a seven-day swim under an ice pack. Instructed by Mother Carey, Tom finds Grimes stuffed to the waist in a prison chimney as punishment for the misdeeds of his previous life. Confronted by Tom, Grimes repents and is freed from the chimney. He is sent off to sweep the crater of Mt. Aetna, and Tom is mysteriously reunited with Ellie on St. Brandon's Isle. During his absence he and Ellie have grown up. As they prepare to enter the world, he as a Carlylean captain of industry and she as his helpmate, they gaze into Mother Carey's eyes. They discover that Mother Carey, the Irishwoman, and all the fairies are identical, and that although there is a further mystery written in Mother Carey's eyes, it is too bright to read.

As a clergyman and amateur naturalist, Kingsley had seen as early as 1843 the approaching conflict between science and religion.[7] However, his acceptance of Paley's rational religion and of Maurice's belief that God is accessible through the faculties of reason and conscience enabled Kingsley not only to attempt to reconcile science and religion but also to welcome scientific discoveries as further revelations of the nature of God.

Believing that matter reflects spirit and that therefore to study matter is to study God, Kingsley believed that fuller knowledge would show science and religion to be compatible even where they appear to conflict. During 1863 Kingsley divided his time between

his parish work and the study of science, and in corresponding with scientific men. Mr. Darwin's "Origin of Species" and his book on the "Fertilization of Orchids," had opened a new world to him, and made all that he saw around him, if possible, even more full of divine significance than before.[8]

The conclusion Kingsley had reached by 1863 as a result of his scientific studies indicates the ways in which he believed science would validate religion. In a letter to Maurice, Kingsley noted that he was "working out points of Natural Theology, by the strange light of Huxley, Darwin, and Lyell." As Kingsley saw it, science was ridding men of "an interfering God — a master-magician, as I call it" and was forcing men "to choose between the absolute empire of accident, and a living, immanent, everworking God."[9]

For Kingsley the eventual reconciliation of science and religion was inevitable: "I agree with Dr. Asa Gray, in his admirable pamphlet on Darwin, that the tendency of physical science is 'not toward the omnipotence of Matter, but to the omnipotence of Spirit.'"[10] To Maurice, Kingsley declared his conviction that "I am sure that science and the creeds will shake hands at last, if only people will leave both alone, and I pray that by God's grace perchance I may help them to do so."[11]

Despite Kingsley's belief that "science and the creeds will shake hands at last," his own view is clearly that of reconciling not two equal contestants but rather the handmaid science to the master religion. Trying to occupy a middle position between "agnostic scientists and suspicious Christians,"[12] Kingsley first accepted the truth of Christianity and then accepted science as revealing material manifestations of that truth.

Mary Wheat Hannawalt says that Kingsley's purpose in *The Water-Babies* was to adapt Darwin's theory of the natural selection of species for children.[13] Kingsley told Maurice that he had

tried, in all sorts of queer ways, to make children and grown folks understand that there is a quite miraculous and divine element underlying all physical nature; and that nobody knows anything about anything, in the sense in which they may know God in Christ, and right and wrong. And if I have wrapped up my parable in seeming Tom-fooleries, it is because so only could I get the pill swallowed by a generation who are not believing, with anything like their whole heart, in the Living God.[14]

The Water-Babies is Kingsley's attempt to illustrate his belief "that the tendency of physical science is not toward the omnipotence of Matter, but to the omnipotence of Spirit."[15] To accomplish this purpose, Kingsley shifted Darwin's idea of natural selection from the physical world to the moral, showing the state of one's physical existence to be dependent on the state of one's soul, and endowed the evolutionary process with a redemptive end. Central to *The Water-Babies* is the theme of moral regeneration and Kingsley's belief that "souls secrete their bodies, as snails do shells."[16] The pattern of Tom's regeneration affirms Kingsley's belief that one's physical state depends upon the condition of his soul.

Tom's regeneration begins before his "death" with the recognition in Ellie's room at Harthover Place that he is dirty. A young chimney sweep whose life has been nasty and brutish, Tom is ignorant of the beauty of nature and of the love of God. Kingsley implies a connection between Tom's inward and outward conditions when the sooty Tom is ashamed of the contrast between himself and the angelically clean Ellie just after only half recognizing a picture of the crucifixion located on Ellie's wall. The next stage of regeneration occurs when Tom follows the sound of churchbells down a mountain and into a valley where he is cared for by a schoolteacher and observed by a mysterious Irishwoman. Another stage occurs when, in answer to the voices of the schoolteacher and the Irishwoman heard in a fevered dream, Tom enters the brook and becomes a water-baby.

Tom's physical regeneration begins with his shame at being dirty; the beginning of his moral regeneration is signaled by his hearing the churchbells. Because his physical regeneration depends upon his moral regeneration, Tom must be reborn. Hence his physical death by drowning is a kind of baptism: the old Tom dies, and the new Tom awakens as a water-baby. His new physical form is not permanent, however; it will evolve as Tom's soul progresses.

In his underwater world, Tom undergoes a variety of experiences, each of which causes his soul to grow. Whatever new self Tom will acquire, he will have to earn. As a willful water-baby, Tom torments many creatures of the sea, failing to perceive the lesson acted out before him when an ugly creature he had been pestering suddenly becomes a beautiful dragonfly. Eventually, however, Tom learns. At considerable risk, Tom rescues a lobster friend from a pot and suddenly discovers that the sea is full of water-babies, whom he had been unable to see or hear. The altruistic act on behalf of the lobster opens his senses and joins him with others of his kind.

Next, Tom comes under the tutelage of Mrs. Bedonebyasyoudid and her kindly sister Mrs. Doasyouwouldbedoneby. These two teachers emphasize the consequences of actions. The first suggests retribution for bad deeds and the second suggests the Golden Rule, holding out the hope of reward for having behaved toward others as one would have them behave toward himself. When Tom stealthily and greedily gulps down Mrs. Doasyouwouldbedoneby's candy, his body grows prickles, taking on a repulsive form consistent with the ugliness of his greed and his betrayal of Mrs. Doasyouwouldbedoneby's kindness. Tom is not beyond redemption, however, for although the fairies make him suffer his prickles as a consequence of his misdeed, they assign Ellie as a tutor to teach him how to be good and thereby to rid himself of his prickles. Through Ellie's assistance and Tom's own determination to be good, Tom need not suffer forever the consequences of his sin. Performing good deeds can save him.

The next stage in Tom's regeneration occurs when Tom is told that if he intends to be a man, he must go out into the watery world alone and aid his old master Grimes, who had drowned while poaching game. Having learned that deeds have consequences and having been instructed by Ellie, Tom must overcome his fear and perform this altruistic task alone. Reluctant to go, Tom is told the morally bracing story of the Doasyoulikes, who did not work at being men and therefore ended their existence as gibbering apes.[17] This story teaches Tom that change is inevitable but that it need not be progressive. Unless Tom works at being a man by performing the moral duties manhood imposes upon him, he may not only cease to grow but also begin to lapse backward into lower forms of life.

Overcoming his fear and repugnance of Grimes, Tom undertakes the search to find his old master. First he locates Mother Carey, who is making things make themselves.[18] Informed by her of Grimes's whereabouts, Tom finds his former master stuck to the waist in a prison chimney. Tom's offer to help Grimes causes the old sweep to repent his mistreatment of Tom and of his own elderly mother. His repentance frees him from the chimney. In a sense, Tom brings full circle the regenerative pattern that had begun when the fairies transformed him into a water-baby. Tom's last lesson reinforces the wisdom of Mrs. Doasyouwouldbedoneby: an action performed in accordance with the way one would like to be treated himself causes one's own soul to grow and may be the cause of growth in that of another. Freed from the chimney, Grimes is sent to the next stage of his own redemption; he must sweep Mt. Aetna. Although Grimes is still being done by as he did, he is, like Tom, being made to make himself.

As Tom and Ellie prepare to return to the world of man, they are granted an insight into the nature of life: the fairy who returns Tom to Ellie is simultaneously the Irishwoman, Mrs. Doasyouwouldbedoneby, Mrs. Bedonebyasyoudid, Mother Carey, and all the other fairies. She is the spiritual reality underlying nature.

The main thread of the plot illustrates Kingsley's belief that the condition of the physical being depends upon the condition of the soul. Furthermore, it demonstrates that the evolutionary process can be directed by exercising moral choice. Altruistic acts performed and duties done cause the soul to grow and hence the body to assume a more attractive form. Tom's development through his several stages into a Carlylean captain of industry makes a resolution familiar to Victorians from Tennyson's *In Memoriam:* directed by moral purpose, which lives at the center of creation, men can rise "on stepping-stones/Of their dead selves to higher things."

Kingsley's friend F. D. Maurice had lost his professorship at King's College as a result of his opposition to the doctrine of eternal punishment, opposition he had recently restated in his *Theological Essays.* Kingsley's sympathy with Maurice's position is evident in *The Water-Babies,* for in this book Kingsley portrays creation as an environment in which spiritual reality directs man's moral evolution; the underwater world is a purgatory, not a hell. Positions in the underwater world, governed by the mysterious Mother Carey, are assigned in such a way as to make the punishment fit the crime. The water-babies are children, like Tom, who have been mistreated or who have died from preventable diseases. In other words, they are children who, having had no chance in life, are remaking themselves under the mystic direction of Mother Carey in her various selves. Other residents of the underwater world, like Grimes, are arranged according to the degree of awareness they had of wrongdoing when they were alive. Even they, however, are not beyond redemption, for Grimes can be genuinely moved to repentance by Tom's kindness and consequently freed from his chimney and set to work on Mt. Aetna while awaiting the next stage in his regeneration. According to Kingsley's understanding of creation and his belief in a loving God, no one undergoes eternal damnation. Through adherence to duty and the performance of purposeful labor, the Divine provides for the regeneration of mankind. It saves, it does not waste, its souls.

Kingsley's preference for applied rather than theoretical science emerges clearly in *The Water-Babies,* a fairy tale in which the science of sanitation is called upon to support the idea that the evolutionary process can be made to serve moral ends. Although Kingsley had treated the science of sanitation in novels and sermons, in *The Water-Babies* he calls upon it to support the principal theme and goes one step further: he shows his skepticism of theoretical science by ridiculing scientists who theorize beyond what he believes are the proper limits of science.

From *Yeast* onward, Kingsley emphasized cleanliness and sanitation. References to personal cleanliness and sanitation abound in his letters and in his works, and water is an item of concern in each of his novels. For example, in *Yeast* the last name of the squire is Lavington and the laborers suffer from typhus; in *Alton Locke,* Jemmy Downs is killed by a fall into an open sewer; and in *Two Years Ago* cholera spreads through a village because the water supply is impure. But bodies of water serve several symbolic ends for Kingsley. For instance, in *Yeast* Tregarva demonstrates his manliness by leaping into a raging stream to rescue the drowning pet of Honoria Lavington, and in *Two Years Ago* Tom Thurnall reenters the novel as the sole survivor of a shipwreck, settling into a new life in Aberalva. The best example, however, of Kingsley's use of water as an archetypal and Christian symbol of rebirth appears at the end of *Westward Ho!,* where the hero, Amyas Leigh, blinded by a lightning bolt during the battle against the Spanish Armada, returns from the sea a chastened man, purged of hatred and prepared to accept the love of Ayancanora.

Kingsley's interest in sanitation and his fascination with water are evident in *The Water-Babies,* whose very title announces his interest. Only a few paragraphs from the beginning a character named Grimes washes his face in a stream. When Tom descends into Ellie's room, he discovers he is dirty. His desire to be clean becomes spiritual as well as physical and drives him into the stream in which he dies to his filthy previous life and, reborn as a water-baby, begins the process of regeneration. As Tom matures and swims toward the sea, the fairies protect him and prevent him from swimming into millraces and sewermouths. When the squire's wife takes children to the seaside, she houses them in "some nasty smelling undrained lodging" and wonders "how they caught scarlatina and diphtheria: but people won't be wise enough to understand that till they are dead of bad smells, and then it will be too late" (XVIII, p. 86). As Tom discovers other water-babies in the sea, he also discovers that their job is to clean rock pools and that they are children who have died of preventable diseases. Furthermore, he discovers that they avoid places where people dump sewage or garbage.

Kingsley's concern with the quality of people's lives was evident in his social novels *Yeast, Alton Locke,* and *Two Years Ago.* In *The Water-Babies,* that concern joined with his lifelong interest in science to suggest that close observation of the natural world would produce knowledge that man could use to improve his lot. Read from one point of view, *The Water-Babies* is a fanciful tract designed to persuade nineteenth-century Englishmen to wash their hands and faces and to clean up their environment. As a sanitation tract, the book advances more fancifully themes introduced in *Alton Locke* and *Two Years Ago*. It teaches Tom Thurnall's lesson that preventable diseases are God's judgment on man's ignorance, for by putting scientific knowledge to work, mankind need not suffer the ravages of typhus, diphtheria, and cholera. *The Water-Babies,* directed at children, conveys this message not to his own generation, but to the next.

Read from another point of view, *The Water-Babies* reveals Kingsley's reservations about science. At stake in this children's story are two principles Kingsley dealt with in his presentation in *Two Years Ago* of the character of Tom Thurnall and was presenting in such books as *Glaucus* and *Madam How and Lady Why*. The first of these principles is that close observation of nature prepares one for life by firmly rooting him in the actual; the second is that learning what one's senses can teach enables him to see that such learning has limitations. The most important limitation is that the most glorious things are not open to the senses and therefore are not open to scientific investigation. Because of this limitation, the scientist should concentrate on studying what he can observe and should not deny the existence of what he has not seen. A scientist who attempts to go beyond this limit makes himself ridiculous. When Tom becomes a water-baby, Kingsley picks up this theme by declaring that the most wonderful things in the world are those which no one can see. This truth, he says, makes nonsense of the claim that because no one has ever seen water-babies they do not exist. It also makes nonsense of the claim that the existence of water-babies is contrary to nature. According to Kingsley two fundamental questions are involved: whether failing to see something proves it does not exist and whether anyone really knows what nature is. Since the answer to both questions is no, one is free to believe in water-babies.

In his treatment of Professor Ptthmllnsprts, Kingsley satirizes a materialist scientist whose analysis of life misrepresents creation because it declares the nonexistence of water-babies solely on the grounds that nobody has ever seen one. Modeled on T. H. Huxley, the professor believes no one should be forced to accept anything as true unless he can see, hear, taste, or handle it. On a trip to the seaside with Ellie, the professor is teaching Ellie about sea life when she announces that there used to be children in the water. She refers for proof to a painting of the phenomenon which is so beautiful it must be true. The professor is unmoved, for he sees no relation between beauty and truth. Ellie is unimpressed by the professor's reasoning and finally asks him why there are no water-babies. The professor replies testily, for lack of a better answer, "Because there ain't" (XVIII, p. 90).

Having just declared that water-babies do not exist, the professor cannot change his mind a few minutes later when he catches Tom, whom Ellie identifies as a water-baby. In Kingsley's mind, the professor's materialist logic holds him to a view of the world that is too narrow to be true. But worse, the professor's logic causes him to reject evidence of the existence of a previously unseen water world even when that evidence is before him. Bolting from the professor in distress at his refusal to admit he was wrong, Ellie drowns. Heartbroken, the professor goes mad, haunted by thoughts that trouble his dreams. Finally, when physicians cannot heal him, the professor heals himself by writing a book contradicting all his previous books. Ridding himself of intellectual pride, the professor becomes a sadder, wiser man and regains his sanity.

This satirical portrait of Professor Ptthmllnsprts reemphasizes Kingsley's fundamentally antimaterialist frame of mind. "Basic to Charles Kingsley's apprehension of nature was the effort to discover God behind mechanism."[19] To the materialism of the professor, Kingsley opposes vitalism; to the professor's view of an orderly nature, Kingsley opposes miracles.[20]

An underlying purpose of *The Water-Babies* is to teach that, unenlightened by the truth of Christianity, the scientific mode offers an inadequate approach to the analysis of nature. To reiterate a point made earlier, Kingsley accepted the truth of Christianity and sought to fit science to his faith.

As a topical fairy tale, *The Water-Babies* has its genesis primarily in the nineteenth-century debate concerning the relationship of science and religion. But it touches a variety of other topics as well. In addition to the principal subjects already discussed, Kingsley also treated two other noteworthy themes. The first of these deals with the employment and mistreatment of children. In 1862 the Second Royal Commission on the Employment of Children was listening to evidence concerning the use of climbing boys.[21] Kingsley's choice of occupation for Tom was probably determined by this evidence. Kingsley's emphasis that the water-babies are children who were mistreated or who died of preventable diseases, however, extends the scope of his concern to condemn other aspects of a social structure that allows its young to be mistreated.

Related to Kingsley's introduction of this theme is his treatment of the second: education and the examination system. In 1861 the Newcastle Commission condemned the inefficiency of primary education and attacked the dames' schools.[22] Kingsley's opposition finds its way into *The Water-Babies* through his presentation in Chapter 2 of the kindly schoolteacher who aids Tom on the night before he drowns. Kingsley's opposition to government interference also takes the form of scattered comments throughout the novel. Kingsley's most successful attack on education, however, concerns the examination system.

In 1860 the Commission on Civil Service had begun to make appointments on the basis of competitive examination. In 1862 Robert Lowe's "Revised Code" introduced to British schools the idea of payment by results. Thus it is that during the 1860s "examination" seemed to be an idol.[23] Kingsley's attack on the idea of examination appears most pointedly when Tom passes the Isle of Tomtoddies, where he finds that the Tomtoddies are all heads and no bodies, that they sing to their idol Examination, and are nervously preparing for their ultimate test by rehearsing a series of pointless questions. In effect the education system is turning children into radishes and turnips.

The evils of physical and academic mistreatment of children and the false guidance of a materialist science join together to destroy in children the imaginative insight which alone can enable them to find God's providence at work in the world. *The Water-Babies,* Kingsley's most fanciful attack on those and other evils, is as much a work of social purpose as anything else he ever wrote. In his historical fiction, Kingsley achieved his social purposes metaphorically by contrasting the past and the present. In turning to Kingsley's historical fiction, one should therefore remain alert to the ways in which nineteenth-century issues are illuminated by the past.

CHAPTER 5

"Past and Present": Historical Novels

FUNDAMENTAL to an understanding of Kingsley's historical novels as "novels of social purpose" is his belief in the providential nature of history. As a Christian, Kingsley believed that God is active in history, directing the affairs of men according to His divine plan toward His desired goal, and that each nation plays a particular role in working out that plan. Kingsley accepted the Bible not only as human history but more importantly as divine history, insofar as he believed the Bible to tell the story of God's continuing revelation of Himself to men. Not to understand that is, for Kingsley, not to understand history.

The sources of the idea are not far to seek. First, Kingsley was an heir to the Christian tradition, within which the idea of the providential nature of history is basic. Second, Kingsley was deeply read in Elizabethan history and literature, where the idea permeates the writing of his favorite poet, Edmund Spenser, and the preface to Sir Walter Raleigh's *The History of the World,* to name but two sources. In Kingsley's own age, Thomas Carlyle taught that history is the message of the past to the present, and, closest to Kingsley's mind and heart, his "dear master" Frederick Denison Maurice, whose influence has been alluded to throughout these pages, preached the providential view of history.

Kingsley's three historical novels portray three crises in world history, in each of which Kingsley believed God had made His will manifest. *Hypatia* (1852) presents the first crisis in the history of Christianity: the conflict of Christianity with Neo-Platonism. *Westward Ho!* (1855) presents a crisis within Christianity itself: the conflict between Protestant England and Catholic Spain. *Hereward the Wake* (1865) portrays the decisive moment in English history between *Hypatia* and *Westward Ho!:* the creation of modern England through the eleventh-century conflict between Norman France and Anglo-Saxon England. Each of these novels represents a critical moment whose resolution marks another stage on the providential journey.

From this perspective, one might consider the three "Condition of England" novels, *Yeast, Alton Locke,* and *Two Years Ago,* as Kingsley's presentation of nineteenth-century crises whose resolution he was attempting to direct according to his understanding of God's intentions revealed in the Bible and by subsequent history. Since each of Kingsley's novels preaches God's active involvement in His creation, it is clear that for Kingsley the principal use of the past is to enable man to understand the present as a part of God's continuing revelation.[1]

Between the writing of *Alton Locke* and *Two Years Ago,* Kingsley produced *Hypatia* and *Westward Ho!,* two of his three historical novels. At odds with what he saw as Manichaean and Neo-Platonic tendencies in his age, Kingsley had struck against them fictionally in *Yeast* and *Alton Locke.* In writing those two novels, he had drawn on a combination of firsthand experience and contemporary reports[2] and had dealt directly with English subjects of immediate concern. But on January 16, 1851, Kingsley wrote to Maurice, informing him that he could write no more on English subjects:

I have exhausted both my stock and my brain, and really require to rest it, by turning it to some new field, in which there is richer and more picturesque life, and the elements are less confused, or rather, may be handled more in the mass than English ones now. I have long wished to do something antique, and get out my thoughts about the connection of the old world and the new; Schiller's "Gods of Greece" expresses, I think, a tone of feeling very common, and which finds its vent in modern Neo-Platonism — anythingarianism.[3]

For some time Kingsley had been thinking about writing a novel along the lines of *Hypatia.* For ten years he had been reading "Monk Latin," and from 1850–1851 he had studied fifth-century Alexandria. Besides *Hypatia,* Kingsley's reading produced two works: *Phaeton; or, Loose Thoughs for Loose Thinkers* (1852), a Socratic dialogue intended to demolish the Neo-Platonic "Anythingarianism" of Ralph Waldo Emerson (represented as Professor Windrush), and *Alexandria and Her Schools* (1854), four lectures delivered at the Philosophical Institute, Edinburgh.

In January of 1852, Kingsley renewed his novelistic attack on Manichaean and Neo-Platonic tendencies in the nineteenth century by beginning the serial publication in *Fraser's Magazine* of *Hypatia; or, New Foes with an Old Face.* In 1853, John Parker, the publisher, issued the work in volume form. From Kingsley's reading of the *Letters of Synesius,* Gibbon's *History of the Decline and Fall of the Roman Empire,*[4] and the *Ecclesiastical History* of Socrates Scholasticus,[5] the "something antique," mentioned in the letter to Maurice, had become *Hypatia*. Conceiving *Hypatia* as a novel of no less purpose than those discussed in Chapter 3, Kingsley attempted to accomplish three major goals. He sought to portray Neo-Platonism as a declining aristocratic philosophy and Christianity as the only truly democratic creed, to denounce asceticism, and to portray the ascendency of Teutonic heroism.

I Hypatia

In the desert near Abbot Pambo's Laura, a retreat at Scetis, Philammon enters the ruins of an ancient temple. He is so awed by the beauty of the place that he wishes to leave the retreat and see the outside world. Reluctantly, Abbot Pambo and Arsenius send him to Alexandria.

In Alexandria, the reflections of the Neo-Platonist philosopher Hypatia are interrupted by the arrival of Orestes, the Roman prefect. Hypatia, who scorns the body as "the prison-house of matter" (IX, p. 18), is especially incensed by Orestes's mention of Pelagia, the courtesan of the Goths. During their discussion of social unrest, Hypatia tells Orestes that

the struggle is simply one between the aristocracy and the mob, — between wealth, refinement, art, learning, all that makes a nation great, and the savage herd of child-breeders below, the many ignoble, who were meant to labour for the noble few. (IX, p. 21)

Departing, Orestes meets Raphael Aben-Ezra, a subtle Jew and the most apt of Hypatia's followers. Raphael adopts a mock-serious Neo-Platonic nonchalance and informs the prefect that Heraclian plans to rebel against Rome.

Meanwhile, Philammon, who is canoeing down the Nile toward Alexandria, is rescued by the Goths from an angry hippopotamus. Aboard the Goths' barge, he is strangely drawn to Pelagia. Putting an oar in Philammon's hands and seeing how well he rows, the Goths, "who, in spite of an occasional inclination to robbery and murder, [are] thoroughly good-natured, honest fellows" (IX, p. 47), clap him on the back in welcome.

With Philammon among the Goths, the scene shifts to Hypatia's chambers, where Hypatia receives a marriage proposal from Orestes. Hypatia does not wish to marry. For the sake of the "good" she might do as empress, however, she consents if Orestes will trample on the cross, restore the Caesareum, and proclaim his contempt for Christianity. Realizing that meeting Hypatias conditions would lead to war with Archbishop Cyril and his monks, Orestes momentarily declines.

Philammon now arrives in Alexandria and is introduced to Cyril and his second in command, Peter the Reader. Joining in a pillaging of the Jewish quarter of Alexandria, Philammon is impressed by Raphael, who suffers his losses with a calm disdain. Later, reflecting on the day's activity, Philammon talks with Peter and with Hieracas, a kindly old priest whose attitudes contrast sharply with Peter's. From Peter, Philammon learns that Raphael is Hypatia's pupil in philosophy. According to Peter, Hypatia is a profligate and her apparent virtues are only "bedizened vices, cunning shams" (IX, p. 103). Philammon's own experience of those virtues as exemplified in Raphael's fortitude, however, does not correspond with Peter's account. He begins to suspect that the monks condemn Hypatia not for what she is but for what they must have her be in order to justify their actions. From Hieracas Philammon receives a commentary on the corruption of the age.

Hieracas laments the passing of the days when Christians were persecuted for their faith. According to him, the church of the present age is too prosperous and is riddled by jealousy and political intrigue. Philammon believes the fault to lie with the enemies of the church and not with the church itself. He concludes that Hypatia is the chief enemy of the church and decides to confront her in her lecture hall. Cyril approves, but warns Philammon not to argue with Hypatia, for she is "subtler than the serpent, skilled in all the tricks of logic" (IX, p. 116).

In the lecture hall on the next day, Philammon shouts that Hypatia's message is blasphemous. But his shout is as much to silence his own doubts as to challenge Hypatia. Almost mesmerized by her beauty and grace, Philammon finds himself for the first time face to face with the "root-questions of all thought" (IX, p. 127).

Once again his experience fails to correspond to the teaching of the Alexandrian monks.

With religious doubts fresh upon him, Philammon returns to the Christian section of the city, hoping for an audience with Cyril. But Peter and the other monks drive him away. Consequently, he goes to Hypatia, begging to become her pupil. Impressed by his earnestness and increasingly tired of the "effeminate selfish triflers" (IX, p. 159) who comprise her audience, Hypatia admits Philammon to her school.

While Philammon is being initiated into the realities of Alexandrian Catholicism, the Goths repose in a splendid house and await the fall of the city and the subsequent opportunity for plunder. Wulf and Smid, the most cunning of the Goths, recognize in Heraclian's rebellion and in Orestes's character signs of decay. Though they long for action and home, they content themselves with wine and heroic stories.

Meanwhile, Raphael, who is in Rome immediately after the failure of Heraclian's rebellion, rises from the ruins "of a doleful fire-scarred tower" (IX, p. 188) to rescue a Christian woman, Victoria, from two ruffians. Victoria's face shines with "clear and joyful determination" and her personality is dominated by "tender and modest thoughtfulness" (IX, p. 201). Moreover, her father is a friend of Augustine of Hippo.

Later, in a fishing boat off the coast of Sardinia, Raphael and Victoria's father discuss religion. Raphael says that he seeks a faith beyond arguments, one that will possess him. Such a faith, he believes, would come to him via such a practical demonstration as the love he observes in Victoria's family. At this point, Raphael entertains the idea that Christianity may be the fulfillment of Jewish national polity. When Victoria's father declares his wish to place his daughter in a convent, however, Raphael scorns the idea that God would derive pleasure from Victoria's celibacy. He falls silent, and, when the boat reaches Berenice, he disappears into the crowd.

In Alexandria, Wulf and Smid propose killing Orestes and helping Philammon remove Pelagia, who Philammon has discovered is his long-lost sister, from the Amal's bed to a desert convent. Once rid of the prefect and Pelagia, they plan to marry Hypatia to the Amal. Then they intend to conquer Africa. That done, Wulf wishes to "try that Red Sea this time — and see Odin face to face, or die searching for him" (X, p. 26).

But Wulf and Smid are not the only plotters in Alexandria. Cyril receives the news of Heraclian's defeat and is advised by Arsenius to keep it quiet, hoping that Orestes will overplay his hand and that the church will gain at his expense. Orestes is incorrectly informed that Heraclian's rebellion has succeeded. He decides to bid for power. Promising to restore the ancient gods, he lures Hypatia to his side and then reveals his plan to win the support of the populace by entertaining them with an elaborate spectacle. Hypatia is disgusted, but consents.

Raphael now joins Synesius, the bishop of Cyrene, in his "fortified country-house" (X, p. 69). Raphael attacks the church's interpretation of the Song of Songs as a justification of celibacy and declares he has come to Synesius because the bishop had married and "stood out manfully" against "this strange modern insanity" (X, p. 75). Synesius suggests that Augustine, expected at any moment, will settle Raphael's spirit.

On the next day, listening to Augustine preach, Raphael is persuaded by the bishop's message of a "Living, Present God, the eternal enemy of discord, injustice, and evil, the eternal helper and deliverer of those who were enslaved and crushed thereby in soul or body" (X, p. 97). Raphael finds that although the message differs from Platonist and Hebrew teaching, it unites and justifies them. Furthermore, he is unable to see any connection between celibacy and the kind of God about whom Augustine preaches.

In the meantime, the Alexandrian spectacle occurs. In the theater, Philammon finds Orestes and Hypatia seated together on the chair of state. As Philammon watches the gladiatorial butchery of the show, he concludes "that luxury, refinement, philosophic culture itself, [are] no safe-guards against the infection of blood-thirstiness" (X, p. 104). The climax of the spectacle occurs when Pelagia performs an obscene dance on the back of a white elephant. As the crowd begins to murmur against the heathenry of what they have seen, Orestes rises to advocate an independent Alexandrian kingdom. A half-hearted few salute him as emperor, and Hypatia kneels before him, ashamed. At this moment, a voice in the back of the theater cries out that Heraclian has been defeated. When the tumult emerges into the street, Orestes finds every church bedecked with placards detailing Heraclian's failure.

Philammon returns to his quarters, where he finds Pelagia repenting her dance. Convincing Philammon that Hypatia participated in the spectacle only because she was forced to, Pelagia begs her brother to intercede for her with Hypatia. Philammon's subsequent discovery that Hypatia has no message for the poor in spirit ends his interest in her philosophy; Philammon's Christianity is reborn as he meditates on its promise of forgiveness.

Deserted by her followers after the spectacle, Hypatia desperately seeks a sign from the ancient gods as a justification of her faith. Failing to obtain one, she prepares to announce her abandonment of philosophy. As she readies herself for the lecture hall, Raphael enters, citing Glaucon and Plato to support his newfound belief that Christianity fulfills philosophy by uniting in the person of Christ both man and God. Hypatia wishes to hear more, but will not be dissuaded from first attending the lecture hall. When she arrives at the hall, she is seized by a mob of angry monks and dragged to the altar of the Caesarium, where she is stripped and dismembered beneath a colossal reproduction of Christ.

With Alexandria collapsing, the major characters still alive begin to leave. Philammon rushes to his sister's quarters among the Goths, where he is forced to kill the Amal in order to capture Pelagia and force her to accompany him to the desert. With the Amal dead, the Goths choose Wulf to be their leader and propose to hack their way through the city and return to their homeland. Before Raphael, too, leaves Alexandria, he has a final interview with Cyril. He angers the churchman by suggesting that once Cyril's work in Alexandria is complete the result will be "the devil's kingdom and not God's" (X, p. 234). With that, Raphael leaves to join his wife, Victoria, in Berenice.

The novel ends with a summary treatment of each of the central characters twenty years after the events described. Cyril is newly dead. But the church of Alexandria had condemned itself even in the moment of its victory. By doing evil that good might come, it had opened itself to a corruption more enervating than Hypatia's philosophy. When the Moslems arrived, the corrupted church fell. Wulf died in Spain as a heathen full of honor. About to be baptized, Wulf had paused and asked the bishop where were the souls of his ancestors:

"In hell," replied the worthy prelate. Wulf drew back from the font, and threw his bearskin cloak around him . . . . He would prefer, if Adolf had no objection, to go to his own people. And so he died unbaptized, and went to his own place. (X, p. 237)

In the desert, Philammon succeeded Pambo as abbot and ruled

with such compassion and understanding that he drew to him the wayward of other monasteries. He was best loved by publicans and sinners and most disliked by religious persons against whose abuses he was ferocious. At night he prayed for two women — one a harlot and the other a heathen. One day Philammon disappeared. He was found in an open grave embracing, as a brother would a sister, a woman of great beauty. On her wrist was a bracelet inscribed "For Amalric Amal's Son Smid Troll's Son Made Me" (X, p. 244).

Hypatia is the best of Kingsley's novels. It is also one of the most often overlooked, critics generally concentrating on the direct social novel *Alton Locke* or the later historical novel *Westward Ho!* Yet in *Hypatia* Kingsley admirably portrays the doubts and dangers of life in an age of transition. He does so on a canvas packed with incidents, themes, and characters which have been carefully organized. Through his handling of characters and themes, Kingsley feelingly develops his conviction that the study of history is the study of God's developing plan, for it finds the spirit of God at work resolving contrarities and conflicts from one age to another and discerns an infinite assurance beneath the temporal storm.

By setting the novel in the fifth century, during the church of the Fathers, that church so admired by Newman and the Tractarians, Kingsley was able to portray at a distance nineteenth-century tendencies which he believed to be destructive of family and national life.[6] To establish Christianity as the only really democratic creed, and philosophy, particularly spiritualism, as the most exclusive and aristocratic, Kingsley portrays a world whose unity is breaking up into cults and parties[7] under the pressure of the Roman collapse, the decline of Greek civilization, a politically ambitious church, and the presence of Teutonic tribes. Principally a novel of initiation and conversion, *Hypatia* is structured in such a way as to fulfill its central purpose by bringing two of its leading characters, Philammon and Raphael, into contact with the contending forces of their day. Important to both young men as they struggle between spiritualism and despair is the doctrine of the Incarnation, which is, according to Kingsley, "morally necessary, to prove the goodness of the Supreme Being."[8] Within the context of *Hypatia,* the Incarnation fulfills philosophy and thereby provides the basis for a more soul-satisfying faith than do the abstractions of Neo-Platonism.

Though not opposites, Philammon and Raphael begin their spiritual journeys from different points and end with an understanding of Christianity which saves them from both spiritualism and despair. Ignorant of the world, Philammon comes to the teaching of Hypatia when he is cast out from the church by the fanaticism of the monks. Weary of the world, Raphael leaves Hypatia's school in despair just as Philammon arrives. What Raphael has learned — that there is great beauty but no hope in Neo-Platonism — is Philammon's lesson by the end of the novel.

Philammon is drawn out of the desert and into the world when he is attracted to the beauty of pagan ruins near his monastic community in the Laura. Suspecting that the world might not be so evil as he has been told, Philammon travels to Alexandria, where he is quickly introduced to representatives of the city's warring parties: Goths, Hypatia and her school, monks, Jews, and Romans. In the clash between Hypatia and the monks, Philammon observes the struggle between Greek intelligence and medieval blindness. Drawn to Hypatia, he is drawn to what remains of the best of the old world. When, as a result of the conflict, Philammon renounces his faith, Kingsley illustrates "a new foe with an old face": loss to the church through the suppression of knowledge.

If the plot is organized to bring Philammon into contact with the contending forces of his day, however, and to draw him toward the best of the old world, it is also designed to return him to Christianity. Most of the events of the novel are arranged for that purpose, but one seems more persuasive than the rest. Philammon's discovery that Pelagia is his sister and that Hypatia has no message for her in her most hopeless state causes the young monk to recall Christianity's emphasis on forgiveness. And so Philammon's return to the church begins through his effort to save his sister's soul. Neo-Platonism ignores the poor and fallen; Christianity does not. Therein Kingsley demonstrates the latter to be the more truly democratic creed.

Still, Philammon's return to Christianity is not a return to the church of Cyril and Peter. In his portrayal of them, Kingsley brings forward at least two more "new foes with old faces": the use of the church for improving one's own worldly condition[9] and the fanaticism of those who embrace Christian symbols without assimilating their spirit. This failure to assimilate the Christian spirit leads the politically ambitious Cyril to use the "devil's tools" and thereby unwittingly to doom his church. Disappointed by both

Cyril's church and by Hypatia's Neo-Platonism, Philammon returns to the desert and attracts to the Laura the wayward and the spiritually troubled. In Alexandria, he loses his innocence, but gains understanding, compassion, and a sense of mission.

Coincident with the story of Philammon's initiation is that of Raphael's conversion. Raphael leaves Hypatia and Alexandria just as Philammon comes to them. Never deeply moved by Hypatia's teaching, Raphael has seemed to toy with it while reserving his powers. Now, his quarters having been sacked by the monks, Raphael, moved by cynical despair, quits the city. Wandering in a spiritual abyss, Raphael meets the beautiful Christian woman Victoria, her father, and eventually Synesius and Augustine. The beauty of Victoria, the loyalty and love exemplified by the members of her family toward each other, and the manliness of Synesius and Augustine convince Raphael to become a Christian. Returning to Alexandria, Raphael is unable to save Hypatia from the monks. Before he leaves for the last time, however, he condemns Cyril's fanaticism. Rejoining his wife in Berenice, he lives out the rest of his days doing good. Like Philammon, Raphael finds an earnest vocation in Christianity and quits Alexandria. The hard-won living faith of neither man can tolerate the blind dogmatism of Cyril and Peter.

In the stories of Philammon and Raphael, Kingsley dramatizes the failure of Neo-Platonism and the success of Christianity in ministering to man's profoundest needs. Each descends into his own spiritual abyss, and each emerges convinced of God's continuing love. In Kingsley's scheme, the Incarnation provides Christianity with its greatest strength, for it is God's assumption of finite form that makes Him knowable. God did not remain an abstract Idea, but acted, became man. This act then became the basis of a faith capable of engaging men's beings, not just their minds. The inability of Neo-Platonism ever to be more than a thought condemns it to failure.

Though not the protagonist and certainly not the most interesting character, Hypatia is nevertheless central to the novel. In the first place, her story focuses Kingsley's major theme: the inadequacy of Neo-Platonism to persons devoid of hope. Through most of the novel, Hypatia dreams of restoring the ancient gods; however, her students — excepting Raphael and Philammon — are effeminate and drawn to her beauty, not to her ideas. Thus, she is nagged throughout by the half-conscious realization that she will fail. After she unwisely joins Orestes, hoping to achieve her goal through an alliance with him, and is humiliated by the Alexandrian spectacle intended to gain popular support for Orestes and herself, she descends into a spiritual abyss akin to those suffered by Philammon and Raphael.

Plagued by self-doubt and by doubts concerning the gods, Hypatia desires a sign from Apollo. When she not only fails to receive one but also is duped by the old Jewess Miriam into mistaking Philammon for Apollo, Hypatia prepares to resign philosophy. As she does so, she is visited by Raphael, who tells her he has found God and man united in Christ. In her despair, Hypatia wishes to hear more; however, before they can meet again, she is dragged by the monks into the Caesarium, hauled before the altar, stripped, and killed. Momentarily, she rises, naked, before a picture of Jesus and raises her arms. The suggestion that Christ accepts her soul is borne out later in a vision which comes to Philammon shortly before his death at the end of the novel. In that vision, Pelegia and Hypatia summon him to heaven.

In the second place, Hypatia is important because around her gather all of the major characters. She is one of the principal opponents of Cyril, she is the friend of Raphael and of Philammon, she is the opposite of Pelagia, she is both the object of Orestes's lust and his reluctant partner in his bid for power, and she is viewed by Wulf and Smid as the one Alexandrian suitable as a wife for the Amal. Still, the action which precipitates events comes, in effect, from outside the story. It is Heraclian's rebellion that brings the Alexandrian hub-bub to a climax. For example, the rebellion causes Orestes to overplay his hand, it causes Hypatia to agree to Orestes's urgings in order to restore the ancient gods, and it brings Raphael and Victoria together.

The stories of the three principal characters support the central theme that Christianity, at least as Raphael and Philammon come to understand it, is a more inclusive creed than Neo-Platonism. Raphael, the Jew, returns to tell Hypatia of his new faith. Philammon's prayers and his vision include both Hypatia, the philosopher, and Pelagia, the courtesan. Hypatia's death at the hands of the monks is, furthermore, the climax of the struggle between ancient intelligence and medieval fanaticism. With Hypatia's death, the best of what remained of the ancient world disappears; with Cyril's victory, the Dark Ages begin.

Like the plots of the social-purpose novels discussed in Chapter

3, the plot of *Hypatia* is packed with characters, incidents, and themes. It is so crowded, in fact, that the story of Raphael Aben-Ezra threatens to break off and become a separate novel. The reasons for this abundance are to be found partly in the Victorian audience's taste for lengthy and elaborate subplots and partly in Kingsley's own intense desire to support his major theme by approaching it in the subplot from a direction different from that taken in the main plot.

In *Hypatia,* Kingsley is especially skillful at grouping his characters in order to elaborate his themes. Consider, for example, Kingsley's presentation of Philammon and Raphael. They are both young; one is a monk, the other a Jew. Both undergo conversion, arriving at a form of Christianity which is "true" and therefore different from the monkish fanaticism of Cyril and Peter. Philammon begins as innocent, Raphael as experienced. Yet, despite contrasts in their backgrounds, each man finds in Christianity a place for himself and work to do. Another group is composed of Hypatia, Pelagia, and Victoria. All three are young and beautiful, and all three point inexorably to messages. Hypatia is a coldly intellectual woman whose spiritual difficulties arise from adherence to a philosophy which teaches her to transcend the physical. The passionate Pelagia, on the other hand, indulges the sensuous at the expense of the spiritual. The ideal is provided by Victoria. As beautiful as Hypatia and as passionate as Pelagia, she is, unlike them, devoutly Christian. Furthermore, although her father wishes to place her in a convent, she wishes to marry. The true expression of her faith comes through marriage to Raphael, who is converted through love of her. Because of her, Raphael becomes a man whose faith and love are expressed in actions, not in thoughts; through marriage to him, Victoria finds fulfillment through an idealized family life. In the establishment of such a family, Kingsley sees the foundation of a new and better society.

The contrasting of Cyril, Peter, and the Alexandrian monks to Pambo, Arsenius, Synesius, and Augustine sets off hard political ambition and fanatical celibacy against a form of Christianity which takes into account the potential goodness of man's physical nature. In the Laura, Pambo and Arsenius are led by reasoning upon their understanding of life to consider marriage as not less holy than celibacy. In another part of the world, Synesius is married and loves sports. Moreover, it is Augustine's full comprehension of human nature that informs his preaching, enabling him to appeal to Raphael and convince him that Judaism is fulfilled by Christianity.

Another of the opposing groups central to the novel is made up of the Romans, the native Alexandrians, and the Goths. The Romans are efficient, but generally unconcerned by riots and murders that do not directly concern them. The principal Roman, the prefect Orestes, is politically ambitious and potentially effective, but impossibly decadent. Years of luxuriant ease in Alexandria have corrupted him. On the other hand, the Alexandrian manhood represented by Hypatia's students is effeminate and disgusting, even to Hypatia. Into this world, ostensibly ruled by a decaying Roman authority, upset by warring factions of monks and Jews, and populated by the effeminate remains of Alexandrian manhood, come the Goths. Large, strong, and physically active, they thrive on sport and combat. Although momentarily made inactive by the enervated Amal, whose potential has been sapped by Alexandrian luxury, they are straightforward rather than subtle or crafty, recognizing worth in a man more by his handling of an oar than by the subtlety of his argument. The future belongs to the descendants of Wulf and Smid, not to the descendants of Orestes or the heirs of Hypatia's thought.

The result of this arrangement is that the characters themselves, as in any novel with a purpose, become embodiments of attitudes or themes. In this regard, Philammon and Raphael are the most persuasive and the most easily associated with characters in Kingsley's other novels. Philammon is a promising, manly youth reared in ignorance but responsive to the influences that pour upon him when he ventures into the teeming life of Alexandria. This combination makes him one of Kingsley's principal spokesmen and gives him a career which resembles that of Alton Locke. On the other hand, the character of Raphael is reminiscent of Lancelot Smith and looks forward to that of Tom Thurnall. Like Lancelot and Tom, Raphael is well educated and capable, a man who suffers not because he lacks earnestness but because he lacks a faith capable of possessing him. Like Lancelot, Raphael eschews celibacy and rescues a beautiful woman from life in a convent. As young men caught up in an age of self-doubt and spiritual uncertainty, Philammon and Raphael are easily as mid-Victorian as they are Alexandrian.

Like Philammon and Raphael, Hypatia illustrates themes, principally the impotence of the Neo-Platonic religion.[10] But unlike them, Hypatia is an historical figure whom Kingsley revised in order to fulfill his fictional purpose. For the exigencies of the plot, Hypatia must be young, beautiful, graceful, and naive; Kingsley made her twenty-five, whereas she was probably in her late fifties or early sixties.[11] In addition, Kingsley shows her presiding over a school composed of perfumed fops, whereas her intellectual gifts were fully developed and the Neo-Platonic school over which she presided was noted for its scholars. Far from being the isolated intellect languishing between effeminate charlatans and the amorous and political advances of the prefect, Hypatia was a prominent citizen often consulted on affairs of state.[12] As a "strong-minded" young Alexandrian-Victorian woman, Hypatia has much in common with Argemone Lavington *(Yeast)* and Eleanor Staunton *(Alton Locke)*. Commenting on possible connections between fifth-century Alexandria and nineteenth-century America, William Dean Howells referred to Kingsley's Hypatia tartly as an "Alexandrian Margaret Fuller."[13]

At the opposite extreme, Pelagia is the Alexandrian sister of the sentimentalized nineteenth-century fallen woman. Although led by circumstances into a life of sportive ease among the Goths, Pelagia is, at heart, a true woman, deeply passionate and capable of a profound and abiding love.[14] Torn between devotion to her brother and love for her Teutonic paramour, Pelagia is eventually ashamed of the life she has led; however, she truly loves the Amal, who dies for her, and she wears his bracelet to the grave. Less inclined to lecture than to love, Pelagia is designed to be an obvious contrast to Hypatia and to be a generally warmer, more sympathetic, because more human, character.

Out of the welter of Alexandrian life portrayed in this novel, the Goths emerge as the group Kingsley most openly admires. Strong and active, Wulf, the central character among them, echoes Tennyson's Ulysses in his urge not to "rust" in Alexandria and in his wish to sail again even if it should mean his death. It is the heroic Wulf, longing for home yet eager to push on beyond Alexandria, contemptuous of Alexandrian manhood and concerned lest his companions weaken through easy living, that Kingsley unashamedly admires. And to Wulf is given the noblest moment in the novel. Having Wulf reject baptism because he prefers to join his ancestors in hell, Kingsley surrounds the old hero with dignity and underscores once more his own disapproval of the doctrine of hell, disbelief in which had recently cost his friend F. D. Maurice his professorship.

II Westward Ho!

In November of 1853, the Russian fleet destroyed a Turkish contingent in the Bay of Sinope. Consequently, the British cabinet decided that to protect their own interests the British and French fleets should enter the Black Sea. In February of 1854, Britain issued an ultimatum: Russia should either evacuate the Turkish possessions of Moldavia and Wallachia by the end of April or prepare for war. By the end of March, war had been declared against Russia, and, although the fighting did not begin until September, British martial spirits ran high.[15] Kingsley's were no exception.

Smarting from the charge of Dr. Pusey and his High-Church supporters that *Hypatia* was an immoral book, Kingsley had maintained a discreet silence. But when his High-Church antagonists' enthusiasm for the Crimean War failed to match his own, Kingsley accused the Puseyites of sympathizing with the Russian Orthodox Church for lack of an attachment with Rome.[16] While Kingsley was most belligerent, J. A. Froude mentioned to him that he was preparing to review a new edition of Hakluyt's *Voyages,* first published in 1582. Kingsley borrowed a volume, and, as he read, the material for *Westward Ho!* took shape.

Reading Hakluyt's epic descriptions, talking to Froude about the Elizabethan age, and living during 1854 in the part of the West Country from whence the sixteenth-century adventurers had sailed convinced Kingsley that the Elizabethan age provided an heroic model for his own. With this model in mind, Kingsley welcomed the Crimean War for the opportunity it provided of recalling to an increasingly materialist and profit-conscious England heroic qualities which he believed had made the nation great. In addition, Kingsley's Elizabethan model justified, for him at least, his admiration of the colonial ruler the Rajah Sir James Brooke, who had been severely criticized in the House of Commons in 1849 for his treatment of the Dyaks. Furthermore, Kingsley's Elizabethan materials enabled him to warn English Protestants of Roman Catholic duplicity following the so-called "Papal Aggression" of 1850. Early in 1855 Kingsley published *Westward Ho!,* noting that it was a most "bloodthirsty" book. The novel was in sympathy with the time and met with instant acclaim.

At the beginning of *Westward Ho!,* Amyas Leigh, the protagonist, is a schoolboy. Reared among ships and sailors and longing to be at sea, he is the symbol of young England longing "to discover and to traffic, to colonise, and to civilise, until no wind can sweep the earth which does not bear the echoes of an English voice" (V, p. 12). But for the time being, Amyas is persuaded to remain in school. Two years later he sets sail around the world with Sir Francis Drake.

When Amyas returns to Bideford at the end of three years, he is an accomplished sailor. Welcoming him home is his brother Frank. Unlike Amyas, Frank is a scholar, a friend of Sir Philip Sidney, and a companion of Continental humanists. Frank is delicate and beautiful; Amyas is huge and strong. Upon returning, Amyas discovers that Rose Salterne, whom he has loved silently during his absence, is lovelier than ever. He also discovers that his Catholic cousin Eustace, educated by Jesuits, has become a sneak. If Frank and Amyas are physical and intellectual opposites, Eustace and Amyas are moral opposites: the one trying to be good by approved methods and rules; the other not knowing whether he is good or not, but doing the right thing instinctively because the Spirit of God is with him. As Amyas renews acquaintances in Bideford, he finds that Mr. Salterne has removed his daughter from the town and that Jesuit priests are skulking about in disguise. Irish troubles are brewing, and Amyas, Frank, Sir Richard Grenvile, Will Cary, and other Bideford notables are worried that the presence of Jesuits in the West Country is part of a Spanish plot to conquer Ireland.

As this episode moves toward its climax, Eustace fails to win Rose. Embittered, he rejoins his Jesuit companions. In the meantime, Amyas and Frank discover that both of them love Rose, and each is determined to stand aside for the other. But war breaks out in Ireland before either can advance his courtship. Meanwhile, Rose is troubled and consults the witch Lucy Passmore, who takes her to Marsland Mouth, where she hopes to provide a vision of Rose's future husband. Failing that, Lucy pacifies Rose by suggesting that perhaps Rose saw no vision because her future husband will be a nobleman from across the sea. Thus is Rose's destiny foreshadowed.

Later, at home Sir Richard Grenvile lectures Amyas on the gospel of labor, warning him away from the selfishness of Puritans, Anabaptists, and Jesuits, whose object in life is to save their own souls:

Amyas, do thou do thy duty like a man, to thy country, thy queen, and thy God; and count thy life a worthless thing, as did the holy men of old. Do thy work, lad; and leave thy soul to the care of Him who is just and merciful in this, that He rewards every man according to his work. (V, p. 152)

As Sir Richard finishes his homily, Salvation Yeo enters the room. Years before, when Sir Francis Drake began his voyage around the world, Yeo had sailed with John Oxenham. Oxenham's ship and crew were subsequently lost.

Newly returned from Spanish captivity, Yeo tells Sir Richard and Amyas the story of the missing crew. He tells how Oxenham and his men went mad with lust for gold and how Oxenham became the cause of shame and ruin. During the journey, Oxenham became enamoured of the wife of Don Francisco Xarate, a Spanish nobleman, and had a daughter by her. Oxenham then proposed settling in the New World instead of returning to England. Before he could carry out his plan, however, Oxenham and his men were captured by the Spanish. Don Francisco's wife subsequently committed suicide, and John Oxenham was hanged, but not before Yeo had promised him never to desert the child. However, Yeo and Oxenham's daughter were separated when he was sent to the Inquisition and from there to service on the galleys. Having escaped from the galleys, Yeo now wishes to join a ship bound for South America, where he hopes to kill Spaniards and search for the child.

Although a voyage to the West must be postponed, Yeo's desire to kill Spaniards can be immediately satisfied, for the Spanish must be driven out of Ireland. But before leaving for Ireland with Yeo, Amyas has unfinished business at home. In gentlemanly fashion, he and Frank had decided that although they both love Rose Salterne, Amyas should have her. Meanwhile, they have discovered that every other young worthy in Bideford also loves Rose. In order to prevent any of the worthies gaining an unfair advantage by being near at hand while the others are killing Spaniards, the group forms The Brotherhood of the Rose, promising thereby to love, but only from afar, for a period of three years.

In Ireland on Christmas night of 1580, Amyas is keeping watch when the Spanish open an offensive which is turned by foul weather and English pluck. Amyas is attacked by a Spanish captain, Don Guzman Maria Magdalena Sotomayer de Soto, whom he captures and returns to camp. There he finds the English commanders debating the treatment of the enemy, who are prepared to surrender. The decision is made: ordinary soldiers are driven from the fort and killed as they emerge. Only the officers are spared:

It was done. Right or wrong, it was done. The shrieks and curses had died away, and the Fort del Oro was a red shambles, which the soldiers were trying to cover from the sight of heaven and earth . . . . It was done; and it never needed to be done again. The hint was severe, but it was sufficient. Many years passed before a Spaniard set foot again in Ireland. (V, p. 244)

An officer, Don Guzman is held for ransom and placed in Amyas's care. Eventually the Spaniard is sent to Bideford to await ransom. For the next two years, Amyas remains at his post in Ireland while Don Guzman secretly woos Rose Salterne.

In 1583, Don Guzman's ransom is finally paid, and he is named Governor of La Guayra in Caracas. Amyas returns to Bideford in time to learn that Rose has eloped with Don Guzman. Her distraught father engages Amyas to go after her. Amyas enlists Salvation Yeo, several members of the Brotherhood, and assorted sailors to accompany him. Following a relatively uneventful voyage, Amyas's ship *The Rose* arrives at La Guayra. In a night maneuver, Amyas and Frank row ashore, locate the governor's palace, and discover Rose and Eustace in conversation. As Amyas and Frank eavesdrop, they are angered by their cousin's villainy. For all of his Spanish shortcomings, Don Guzman genuinely loves Rose and has sworn to respect her Protestantism. Eustace, however, poisons their marriage by attempting to convert Rose to Catholicism and by convincing Don Guzman that she longs for her English lovers. Amyas and Frank realize too late that their presence plays into Eustace's hands. Discovered, Frank and Amyas run for the beach; Amyas is knocked cold and rescued by members of his crew. Frank, wounded, is left behind.

Back aboard *The Rose,* Amyas and his men fight their way past three Spanish ships, but *The Rose* is severely damaged. Finding a harbor near La Guayra, Amyas puts in for repairs only to have the crew come down with fever. Realizing *The Rose* cannot be repaired, Amyas orders that the ship be burned and that the crew move inland in search of treasure and El Dorado. While Amyas and his crew contend with their jungle adventures, Frank and Rose, betrayed by Eustace, die in the Inquisition. Eustace subsequently disappears from the novel: "This book is a history of men . . . and

Eustace is a man no longer; he is become a thing, a tool, a Jesuit
.... We have no more concern with Eustace Leigh" (VI, pp. 120-21).

At the end of three years, Amyas's crew, disappointed in their
search for cities of gold, decide to raid the Spaniards, steal a ship,
and return to England. With this plan in mind, they set off to find
the Spaniards and the seacoast. On their way, they encounter an
Indian tribe. One of the Indians, a girl named Ayancanora, falls in
love with Amyas.

Wishing to enlist the aid of the Indians in attacking the Spaniards, Amyas and his men settle near them for a time. As they become better acquainted with the Indians, Amyas notices that
Anancanora sings like a European. Amyas's mind, however, is on
fighting Spaniards, and he thinks no more about it. When the
Indians agree to help, he is cheered. But his joy is tempered; although the Indians will let Amyas's crew have the gold, they wish
to eat the Spaniards. The English therefore decide to carry on
alone.

Soon after, the English locate a Spanish contingent which is simultaneously transporting treasure and mistreating women and
slaves. Once again recognizing Spanish villainy and responding to
their knowledge that the instinct for freedom is the righteous voice
of God, the Englishmen do their duty. When they have slain the
Spaniards and claimed the treasure, they discover that Ayancanora
not only has followed them but also has joined the battle. After the
battle, Amyas leaves the freed slaves in the care of a kindly Spanish
hermit and pushes on.

Eventually the Englishmen capture a Spanish ship and undertake
their homeward voyage. When the ship's hold is emptied of its
prisoners, the English discover Lucy Passmore, the witch of
Devon. From her they learn that Rose and Frank died in the Inquisition, condemned by the very bishop aboard the ship they have just
captured. Amyas orders the bishop and an accompanying friar to
be hanged. From the Spanish captain, Amyas learns that Don
Guzman has returned to Spain. From Lucy, he also learns the full
evil of Eustace, who had brought his Jesuitism between Don
Guzman and Rose.

Meanwhile, the English crew is amazed when Ayancanora joins
them in their songs. As her sleeping memories awaken, Salvation
Yeo realizes that she is "the little maid" whom he has been seeking.
If this knowledge overpowers Yeo, it works miracles on
Ayancanora, who now decides to become civilized and to be

worthy of her English heritage. But the discovery hardens Amyas against her, for although Ayancanora is half English, she is also half Spanish.

Arriving home with fewer than half the men who set out with him, Amyas discovers that Mary Queen of Scots has been executed, learns of Sir Walter Raleigh's adventures in North America, and inherits Mr. Salterne's estate on the condition that he rechristen his ship *The Vengeance*. In 1588, Amyas is eager to join the fleet and to battle the Armada, for he knows that Don Guzman must be aboard one of the ships. Throughout the battle, Amyas is consumed by the desire to kill Don Guzman. At the end of the last day's battle, Amyas follows his retreating adversary into the stormy seas. Praying that God will permit him to kill Don Guzman, Amyas appears to be possessed by a devil. About to close on his enemy, Amyas is frustrated by the storm, which drives the Spanish ship onto the rocks. Angry that their revenge has been thwarted, Amyas and Yeo are struck by lightning; Yeo is killed, and Amyas is blinded.

Amyas eventually accepts his blindness as God's judgment on his hatred of the Spanish. He concludes he was correct to fight, but wrong to hate. Thus at peace with himself, Amyas is reconciled with Don Guzman in a dream. With that reconciliation comes another: Amyas accepts the love of Ayancanora, who sinks with a sob onto his bosom.

Although *Westward Ho!* was an immediate success, at least two contemporaries did not care for it. Henry Crabb Robinson noted in his diary that it was one of Kingsley's "least agreeable" novels, and George Eliot wrote in the *Westminster Review* that, as usual, Kingsley's parsonical habit spoiled his book: "Kingsley sees, feels, and paints vividly, but he theorizes illogically and moralises absurdly."[17] In the twentieth century readers have found *Westward Ho!* to be the "most generally readable" of Kingsley's novels,[18] the closest thing to a novel he ever wrote,[19] or even the best book Kingsley wrote,[20] the "pinnacle of his achievement."[21] But at least one modern critic finds it difficult to believe that *Westward Ho!* was ever intended for adults.[22]

In *Hypatia,* Kingsley draws parallels between the spiritual confusion of fifth-century Alexandria and that of nineteenth-century England. In *Westward Ho!,* he draws correspondences between the adventures of sixteenth-century English heroes on the Spanish Main and the adventures of nineteenth-century Englishmen in the

Crimea. Believing in the providential nature of history, Kingsley taught that individuals and nations doing their duty serve a cause larger than they can realize at the moment.

For Kingsley, as for many Victorians, the word *duty* conveys a transcendental sense of mission that it has since lost. In Kingsley's terms, to flinch from the performance of duty is to abdicate a divine responsibility and to open the world to tyranny or to chaos. *Westward Ho!* conveys Kingsley's lesson to the generation at war in the Crimea by linking particular events — the search for Rose Salterne, for example — to the larger, less conscious cause of guaranteeing the freedom of the seas and making the world safe for Protestantism. In short, Kingsley intended *Westward Ho!* to steel English nerve by portraying as divinely sanctioned England's role in world affairs.

Westward Ho! could be considered Kingsley's epic, for it conveys through an episodic plot the sense of a divinity working out his plans through larger-than-life heroes whose arena is the world. At issue is a nation's fulfillment of its destiny. The plot of *Westward Ho!* consists of episodes, a series of adventures held together by the presence of the central characters and by the increasing seriousness of the enmity with Spain that concludes with the defeat of the Armada. But *Westward Ho!* presents several of Kingsley's other major themes as well: the sanctity of the home, the morally uplifting value of woman, the cunning and duplicity of Catholicism, and the virtues of muscular Christianity are among the foremost. Furthermore, *Westward Ho!* follows the pattern of characterization familiar by now: the characters represent spiritual positions and are arranged as foils or opponents to a protagonist in order to point a moral.

In *Westward Ho!,* the characters are both historical and fictional, with the fictional characters appearing at the center of the story. Among the historical characters are Sir Philip Sidney, Edmund Spenser, Sir Francis Drake, and Sir Richard Grenvile. A felt presence though she never appears, Queen Elizabeth inspires the accomplishments of her heroes, retaining for Kingsley her Spenserian value as "Gloriana." The principal fictional characters are Amyas Leigh, the protagonist; Frank Leigh, his courtly brother; Eustace Leigh, Amyas and Frank's Jesuit cousin; Salvation Yeo, an Anabaptist loyal to Amyas; Don Guzman, Amyas's Spanish antagonist; Rose Salterne, the Bideford beauty around whom is formed the Spenserian Brotherhood of the Rose; and

Ayancanora, the "little maid" whose discovery is the object of Yeo's journey. Although the female characters in *Westward Ho!* are relatively insignificant in themselves, they are central to the novel in that they inspire the men. The fact that women are central to the novel without being frequently present indicates that in *Westward Ho!* Kingsley is concerned with the "meaning of woman," not with highly individualized female characters.

The characters and events of the novel comprise four overlapping spheres of influence. The most inclusive sphere consists of the historical and fictional English characters. At its center, is Queen Elizabeth, love and admiration for whom motivates the grand action of the plot which ends in the sinking of the Armada. Another sphere comprises the fictional English characters at whose center is Rose Salterne, love and admiration for whom activates The Brotherhood of the Rose to perform heroically against Spain, unconsciously supporting the grand action. Salvation Yeo's dedication to the "little maid" forms a smaller circle within this one, for Yeo travels with Amyas, and his devotion to Ayancanora encourages his heroism in concert with that of Amyas. The third and fourth spheres are, of course, the Spanish ones. At the center of the more inclusive Spanish sphere is not chivalrous love for a woman, but the Inquisition and lust for world domination. At the center of the lesser sphere is Don Guzman's well-intentioned but fatal love for Rose Salterne, a love poisoned by Jesuitry.

Kingsley's admiration of physical strength, often at the expense of intellectual accomplishment, is one of the hallmarks of his fiction. For example, it appears in *Yeast* in the character of the healthy foxhunting of Lancelot Smith and the physique of the gamekeeper Tregarva. It appears again in the character of Tom Thurnall in *Two Years Ago,* and it appears in *Hypatia* in Kingsley's treatment of the Goths. In *Westward Ho!,* it appears most particularly in the character of Amyas Leigh, who is set off by contrast to a number of foil characters. Amyas's qualities are highlighted first by contrast with those of his brother Frank. A practical man, Amyas quits school as soon as he is allowed to and sails around the world with Sir Francis Drake. He is consistently described in terms of his physical strength; he is, put simply, a "blond giant." He is intuitively shrewd and is clearly meant to lead an active life. On the other hand, Frank is a courtier, the companion of Continental humanists. He is consistently described in terms of physical weakness and his intellectual and diplomatic skills. Fond of euphuistic

speeches and delighting in elaborate metaphors, Frank is the moti-
vating genius of The Brotherhood of the Rose; it is his idea which
unites the young Bideford worthies through courtly devotion to
Rose Salterne.

Despite Kingsley's portrait of Frank's courtly beauties, he clearly
prefers Amyas's unreflective vigor. This point is emphasized when
Amyas gathers his crew and prepares to sail in search of Rose.
Amyas receives a note from Sir Francis Drake concerning a project
for providing Plymouth with clean drinking water. In response,
Frank composes "a pretty epigram, comparing Drake's projected
leat to the river of eternal life whereof the just would drink
throughout eternity" (VI, p. 18). Amyas pays more heed to an
appendage scrawled onto Drake's letter by John Hawkins and offering advice on the mounting of ordnance and the use of vitriol in
place of fruit to combat scurvy. As Frank watches his brother
during the following months, he is humbled:

For he watched with astonishment how the simple sailor, without genius,
scholarship, or fancy, had gained, by plain honesty, patience, and common sense, a power over the human heart, and a power over his work,
whatsoever it might be, which Frank could only admire afar off.
(VI, p. 19)

Frank's courtly graces and his learning bow to Amyas's practical
instinct and his sailor's skill.

Although Frank's regard for his own abilities shrinks as a consequence of watching his brother prepare for the voyage, it is clear
that he is courageous. In the Inquisition, Frank refuses to recant his
Protestantism and dies at the stake with Rose, who likewise refuses
to recant. The two of them, the euphuistic courtier and the lady
who provided him with his courtly ideal, die as witnesses to their
English Protestantism and gain thereby a nobility which they had
lacked. In choosing to participate in the search for Rose and in
bravely facing death, Frank becomes less the euphuistic scholar,
whose product is witty epigrams, and more the active hero, whose
product is duty done, the weak defended, and the seas kept open
for British trade. Frank's courtliness and the manner of his death
highlight Amyas's character, emphasizing the superiority of
Amyas's practical intelligence and the value of courage.

Another character who acts as a foil to Amyas is the sailor Salvation Yeo. He is intended to be, as Stanley Baldwin points out, a

type of the best English sailor of the Elizabethan age: daring, courageous, and loyal.[23] When Yeo first enters the story, he is an established sailor freshly home from a successful voyage, and Amyas is a boy wishing to go to sea. Between this appearance and the next, Yeo undergoes a disastrous voyage with John Oxenham, separation from the "little maid," whom he has sworn to protect, torture in the Inquisition, and finally forced service in the Spanish galleys.

When Yeo reappears, he is a changed man. He is grim, humorless, and intent on finding "the little maid" and on killing Spaniards. When he joins Amyas, both are seeking women for whom they feel responsible; Yeo seeks "the little maid" because of an oath sworn years before, and Amyas seeks Rose because he loves her and because of his vow as a member of the Brotherhood of the Rose. When Amyas learns that Frank and Rose have been killed in the Inquisition, he becomes, like Yeo, grim and determined to gain revenge. At this point, Yeo's madness highlights that of Amyas, and the two men become illustrations of Kingsley's lesson that although fighting tyranny is the cause of God, personal enmity is the cause of the Devil.[24]

Kingsley's portrayal of Amyas, Frank, and Yeo emphasizes their chivalry, their belief in the sanctity of their home and their country, and their adherence to their duty. The villainy of Eustace Leigh contrasts with these virtues. In his portrayal of Eustace, Kingsley dramatizes Catholic cunning and duplicity which he believes undermine the love of men and women and thereby destroy the home, that most sacred of Victorian institutions. Eustace is typecast. He is a static character, a lustful coward who embodies Jesuit villainy, and treachery of the lowest sort: he betrays a woman and a relative. Although he is not in the story very much, he is necessary to it, for it is either through or by him that the villainy is committed which moves the plot.[25]

As a youth, Eustace was sent to Rheims to be trained as a seminary priest, "in plain English, to be taught the science of villainy, on the motive of superstition" (V, p. 62). Eustace was a quick study, and was returned to England by his superiors because of his

"peculiar vocation"; in plain English, because the wily priests had seen in him certain capacities of vague hysterical fear of the unseen (the religious sentiment, we call it now-a-days), and with them that tendency to be a rogue, which superstitious men always have. (V, p. 63)

Eustace's Jesuit education turns him into "a very fair liar" and, as such, the sort of tool his superiors want in England.

Eustace's Jesuit training enables him to understand neither women nor love:

> he looked on her [Rose] as a lamb fallen unawares into the jaws of the greedy wolf, which he felt himself to be. For Eustace's love had little or nothing of chivalry, self-sacrifice, or purity in it; those were virtues which were not taught at Rheims. (V, p. 77)

Having been taught that all love is lust, Eustace longs with "a wild selfish fury" (V, p. 77) to marry Rose. When she rejects his vulpine proposal, he is maddened by his frustrated sexuality and tells her that she will regret her refusal.

Following Rose's marriage to Don Guzman, Eustace is attached to their household in South America. There, Eustace undermines Don Guzman's love of Rose by arousing in him petty jealousies and fears that turn him against her. When Eustace discovers that Frank and Amyas have come to La Guayra, he turns their visit against her, delivering Rose and the captured Frank to the Inquisition. Then, overcome by self-contempt, Eustace requests and is granted a transfer. With that, Kingsley declares that Eustace has ceased to be a man and sends him out of the novel.

Except for Eustace Leigh, the English characters are admirable. The Spanish are quite another matter. Whether Amyas finds Spaniards in Ireland or in the New World, they are vain-glorious, hot-tempered, and insolent; but they are not without the fundamental courage and skill which make them ferocious opponents. The basic difference between the Spaniards and the English, as Kingsley portrays them, is that Spain seeks to reduce the world to servitude, whereas England seeks to defend free trade and free seas for all the world. This fundamental difference between the two nations is portrayed throughout *Westward Ho!,* but in no section more clearly than in Chapter 25, "How They Took the Gold Train."

As Amyas and his crew prepare to ambush a Spanish gold train, they hear a cracking sound and a loud cry of pain:

> "That was a whip's crack," said Yeo, "and a woman's wail. They are close here, lads!"
> "A woman's? Do they drive women in their gangs?" asked Amyas.

"Why not, the brutes? There they are, sir. Did you see their basnets glitter?" (VI, p. 168)

Appearing on the trail is a troop of Spaniards, who are forcing slaves to carry baskets of gold. The slaves have been scarred by whips and fetters and are chained together in a line.

The English are particularly enraged when they observe not only "old men and youths among them, but women; slender young girls, mothers with children running at their knee." Fortunately for the slaves, the English utter

a low murmur of indignation . . . worthy of the free and righteous hearts of those days, when Raleigh could appeal to man and God, on the ground of a common humanity, in behalf of the outraged heathens of the New World; when Englishmen still knew that man was man, and that the instinct of freedom was the righteous voice of God . . . . (VI, pp. 169–70)

As the troop arrives at a log felled across the path by the English, the Spaniards order the slaves to clear the way. One of the slaves collapses and is unable to rise. A soldier then cuts off the offender's hand, whereupon a young girl knocks the soldier over the edge of a cliff, but falls with him and is left dangling by her hand. As the angry Spaniards pull her to the top in order to avenge the death of their comrade, Amyas and his men attack. The fight is brief and its outcome sure. Once the English have killed the Spaniards they enlist the aid of the slaves in carrying the gold down the mountain, promising to free them at the journey's end.

In this episode, justice is served by English sailors, whose sensibilities having been aroused by the Spaniards' treatment of Indians, intervene on the side of God and common decency. Were it not for such English intervention, evil would be perpetuated and the world enslaved. This episode illustrates Kingsley's providentialism, for in one stroke it justifies Elizabethan piracy, imperial expansion, and the Crimean War.

Nevertheless, regardless of the cruelty of the Spanish soldiers, the most inexcusable acts are reserved for the Spanish clergy. This is so because Kingsley wishes to portray the effect on the mass of men when Christianity is corrupted and reduced to rule. In essence, the cruelty of the Spanish soldiers is caused by the perverse guidance of their Catholic faith as taught by Jesuits and as enforced by the Inquisition. This point is at the center of Chapter 26, "How They Took the Great Galleon."

Aboard the galleon *The City of the True Cross,* the Bishop of Carthagena gazes toward the shore and reflects on the recent sacking of his cathedral town by Sir Francis Drake. He discourses on the vanity of riches and the snare of wealth and asks with unintentional irony, "Who knows better than I, how much human nature lurks in us fallen sons of Adam?" (VI, p. 198). As the evening wears on, the wine flows freely, and the bishop admits that whatever the fate of his see he has managed to save "somewhat . . . from the general wreck" (VI, p. 203). With a reminder that life is short, the bishop dismisses the others and retires.

His sleep is interrupted when two servants attempt to murder him. Their plan is spoiled by Amyas's capture of the galleon. When the English discover victims of the Inquisition in the ship's hold, Amyas learns that the same bishop whose pieties we have overheard is responsible for the operation of the Inquisition as well as for the enslaving and murdering of Indians. It is he who condemned Rose and Frank. The bishop has used the church to gain power and prestige and has then used that power and prestige to oppress others. His pieties are conventional and without substance. The English hang him.

Pernicious doctrines preached by self-serving clerics blight the fiber of a nation and thereby ruin potentially honorable men. Kingsley illustrates this belief through his portrayal of two men, the commandant of the captured galleon and Don Guzman. Following the hanging of the bishop, Amyas and the Spanish commandant converse briefly. Agreeing that Amyas's hanging of the bishop is just, the commandant attempts to exculpate himself in Amyas's eyes. He describes the effect of the Inquisition on the people of Spain:

This Inquisition is the curse of us, the weight which is crushing out the very life of Spain. No man dares speak. No man dares trust his neighbour, no, not his child, or the wife of his bosom. It avails nothing to be a good Catholic, as I trust I am . . . when any villain whom you may offend, any unnatural son or wife who wishes to be rid of you, has but to hint heresy against you, and you vanish into the Holy Office . . . . (VI, p. 225)

His face working convulsively, the commandant reveals to Amyas that his own sister had gone into the Inquisition nine years before and had not been heard from since. Horrified, Amyas asks whether the commandant has avenged her. The commandant replies that killing a churchman would send him to the stake and to hell: "when I saw you just now fearing those churchmen no more than you feared me, I longed, sinner that I am, to be a heretic like you" (VI, p. 226). When Amyas suggests that the commandant is not far from being "a heretic, as you call it — a free Christian man, as we call it" (VI, p. 226), the commandant crosses himself fervently. He declares that his duty is obedience and that the Church's authority is infallible.

In this brief scene, Kingsley dramatizes his belief that England's struggle is not only on behalf of free seas and free trade but also on behalf of free minds and free spirits. Instinctively kind and courageous, the commandant's humanity is circumscribed by Catholic doctrines which join temporal to spiritual fear, bending men to obedience. As a result, the Christian love and the righteous anger of a nation are curbed, and the Inquisition is perpetuated.

The only fully developed Spanish character in the novel is Don Guzman, the paradigm of a cunning Spanish nobleman whose faults are sufficiently relieved by his valor to make him attractive. Whatever else he is, Don Guzman is not treacherous.[26] Kingsley establishes the Don's character within a few pages of his capture by Amyas Leigh during the Irish wars. Subsequent events confirm rather than develop it. Don Guzman exhibits impressive physical beauty and graceful demeanor, and Amyas is "thrown off his balance" by Don Guzman's "unexpected assurance and cool flattery" (V, p. 235).

Physical beauty, courage, and a suave bearing are not, however, all there is to Don Guzman. A less flattering side is revealed to the reader, if not to Amyas, when the Don discovers that he had lost his sword during the skirmish of the previous night:

A flash passed over the Spaniard's face, which disclosed terrible depths of fury and hatred beneath that quiet mask, as the summer lightning displays the black abysses of the thunderstorm; but like the summer lightning it passed, almost unseen . . . . (V, p. 237)

As soon as Amyas leaves, Don Guzman plunges "into the inner tent, stamping and writhing, gnawing his hands with rage and shame." There is in Don Guzman awareness of his station, strong pride, and a frightening depth of passion.

Don Guzman's pride and stateliness are mingled with callousness and toleration of cruelty, for he is capable of chatting as idly about the murder of women and children as about the treasures to be plucked from along the Amazon. The English, particularly Amyas, respond to Don Guzman with a mixture of fascination and disgust, eventually rejecting him. The Spaniard — represented by Don Guzman — is too calculatingly cool, too ready to accept cruelty without question, and too secretive about his intentions in the New World for the modest and sober Englishman — represented by Amyas Leigh — to trust completely.

The fatal weakness of Don Guzman, like the weakness of Spain itself, is overweening pride mixed with toleration of cruelty. This weakness transforms Amyas's reservations about the Don into hatred when he discovers that the Spaniard has permitted the delivery of his wife to the Inquisition. From this point on, national rivalry between England and Spain as it is figured in the characters of Amyas and Don Guzman, becomes an excuse for personal enmity, and the world becomes their personal battlefield. Only the death of the Don in a stormy sea and the blinding of Amyas by a bolt of lightning — acts of nature interpreted as God's judgment on the personal animosity of both — can reconcile them and point the moral: God may sanction the English cause, but He reserves vengeance to Himself.

Unlike their male counterparts, the female characters of *Westward Ho!* are relatively minor figures. Their presence is pervasive, to be sure, but fundamentally as an ideal capable of inspiring men to perform heroic acts. Queen Elizabeth exists as a sort of Spenserian Gloriana or as an "eternal feminine" who draws England's men on to a greatness otherwise unachievable. Only the characters of Rose and Ayancanora are developed significantly.

For the sake of the plot, Rose must be capable of causing all the eligible young men of Bideford to fall in love with her. Consequently, she is all that one expects: she is young, beautiful, and romantic. She is also courageous and strongly Protestant, but not so patriotic as to consider Don Guzman ineligible solely because he is a Spaniard.[27] The young Bideford worthies make Rose the unwitting central figure in their Spenserian Brotherhood of the Rose and swear to worship her from afar for three years. Rose, meanwhile, insists on behaving as a real woman. Thus, while the Bideford worthies, inspired by the romantic conception of the Brotherhood, win their fame in war and diplomacy abroad, Rose is swayed by Don Guzman at home. Although a modern reader may be inclined to cheer when Rose elopes with Don Guzman and escapes the tedious attention of the Brotherhood,[28] the significance of the event is not that it frees Rose, but that it focuses the plot. What had been a novel consisting of separate adventures and apparently unrelated wars becomes the story of a purposeful search and a lesson learned. Rose is not actually present very often, but her actions in concert with those of Don Guzman join with the Brotherhood's idealizing of her to determine the direction of the story.

Like Rose, Ayancanora has inspirational value, but unlike her she is tangential to the plot even while lending it interest and assisting in bringing it to a satisfying conclusion.[29] Ayancanora is attached to the plot through Salvation Yeo, who knows her only as his "little maid." Believing that his oath to protect the "little maid" binds him to a sacred duty, Yeo cannot rest until he locates the girl and knows her fate. Thus, his search for Ayancanora parallels Amyas's search for Rose.

Furthermore, the story of Ayancanora parallels the main plot in another, perhaps less direct, way. Ayancanora is the daughter of John Oxenham and a married Spanish noblewoman with whom he eloped. Yeo's determination to locate Ayancanora permits his telling the tragic love story of the English captain and the Spanish lady shortly before Kingsley introduces Don Guzman. Before Don Guzman and Rose meet, therefore, Kingsley has prepared his readers for a tragic affair between Spanish and English lovers. Also, Amyas's end-of-the-novel acceptance of Ayancanora's love permits Kingsley to end the novel satisfyingly by showing Amyas to have been reconciled to Don Guzman and to Rose and finally to have found peace.

Also, Ayancanora's story shows Kingsley's typical Victorian acceptance of racist ideas, for telling it enables Kingsley to comment on differences between Indians and the English, at the expense of the former and to the glorification of the latter. After an initial meeting with Ayancanora, Amyas and his crew find her being worshipped by her tribe as the Daughter of the Sun. They are amazed to find that she sings like a European in a voice so rich that the Indians bow in awe before her. Later, the English sing psalms in their camp and are astonished to hear her mimicking them from the forest. During a dispute between the Indians and the English, Ayancanora sides with the English:

"I am a daughter of the Sun; I am white; I am a companion for Englishmen! But you! your mothers were Guahibas, and ate mud; and your fathers — they were howling apes!" (VI, p. 153)

When Amyas follows this outburst by kicking an offending Indian, Ayancanora sulks and the other Indians burst out laughing "like grown-up babies." Later, sailing back to England, Ayancanora, who has been trying with little success to assume the manners of an English lady, discovers her identity:

The thought that she was an Englishwoman; that she, the wild Indian, was really one of the great white people whom she had learned to worship, carried in it some regenerating change: she regained all her former stateliness, and with it a self-restraint, a temperance, a softness which she had never shown before. (VI, p. 245)

Through his contrasting portrayal of Ayancanora among the Indians and among Englishmen, Kingsley illustrates his belief that to be English, and to be aware of the fact, is to wish to take one's proper place. It is therefore suitable to Kingsley that Ayancanora be not a real Indian, but the daughter of an English gentleman and a Spanish noblewoman. As such, she can be acceptable to Amyas, and their reconciliation at the end can resolve Amyas's internal conflicts and symbolize his inner peace. The romantically idealized Rose Salterne does not provide such possibilities.

III Hereward the Wake

Between the publication of *Westward Ho!* in 1855 and the serial publication in the periodical *Good Words* of *Hereward the Wake, "Last of the English"* in 1865, Kingsley published a variety of work. In 1856 *The Heroes; or, Greek Fairy Tales for my Children* appeared. In 1857 *Two Years Ago* was published; in 1858 *Andromeda and Other Poems* appeared. The years 1859–1861 are remarkable not for the publication of any major work, but for the breadth of interest his titles indicate. There are, of course, sermons, but there are also prefaces to historical books, poems, the lecture titled "The Limits of Exact Science as Applied to History," and new editions of earlier works. In 1862 *The Water-Babies: A Fairy Tale for a Land Baby* began appearing serially in *Macmillan's Magazine;* in 1863 *The Water-Babies* was concluded in its serial format and was issued in book form. The year 1864 is notable for at least two items: it was the year *The Roman and the Teuton* lectures were published, and it was the year of "What, Then, Does Dr. Newman Mean?"

Kingsley's first historical novel, *Hypatia,* had been attacked by the High-Church party, but his second, *Westward Ho!,* had been widely admired. In spite of their "crudities and occasional anachronisms," these novels exhibited a "truly sensitive historical understanding . . . for the atmosphere and life of two different ages."[30] In 1854 Kingsley published "a genuine work of historical study, *Alexandria and Her Schools,* . . . a book which was one of the first in the English language seriously to sketch the continuity of Neoplatonic and Christian thought in a sympathetic spirit."[31] On the basis of these works and because of royal favor, Kingsley was offered the Regius Chair of Modern History at Cambridge in 1860.

At Cambridge in the 1860s Kingsley revived his acquaintance with the fens. On a trip to Crowland Abbey near Peterborough in the summer of 1848, Kingsley had been impressed by the abbey, by the fens, and by the lowland populace. In the intervening years, he had written of the fens in his prose idylls and had come to believe that the lowland dwellers had been inadequately dealt with in literature. Cambridge provided access to the fens and to source material for *Hereward the Wake.* As Kingsley's footnotes and allusions insist, *Hereward the Wake* is a heavily researched novel. The principal sources are the *Anglo-Saxon Chronicle,* Geoffrey of Gaimar's *Metrical Chronicle,* the *Life of Hereward* written by Hereward's house priest Leofric, and the fragmentary *The Family of Hereward,* edited by Thomas Wright.[32]

In *Hereward the Wake* the familiar themes appear. Kingsley reaffirms his belief in the ennobling effect on a man of the love of a good woman and dramatizes his conviction that the loss of self-respect is fatal to one's noblest efforts. The homiletic digressions, familiar from the earlier works, are kept to a minimum in this the last and most straightforward of Kingsley's novels.

Hereward, the second son of Earl Leofric and Lady Godiva and brother-in-law to King Harold, is an uncontrollable eighteen-year-old in 1054. He is strong, full-chested, and blond, but because he wastes his strength in living riotously and in bullying monks, he is outlawed by his pious mother. Hereward is joined in exile by

Martin Lightfoot, a mad but adventurous member of Lady Godiva's household.

In the company of Gilbert of Ghent in the north of England, Hereward fights Celts, hunts deer, and becomes a favorite with the ladies. His special friend is Alftruda, a ten-year-old girl who is beautiful, precocious, and vain. In her defense Hereward accomplishes the first of his heroic acts. Gilbert keeps a polar bear, which Hereward has unsuccessfully begged to fight. One day as Hereward and Martin return from a hunt, they find the bear loose in the streets and menacing Alftruda. Felling the beast with a single stroke, Hereward makes his name and saves the child. In the enthusiasm of the moment, Hereward's Viking blood is aroused, and he believes that his career may eventually rival that of mythic heroes such as Beowulf.

Hereward's slaying of the bear fires the jealousy of Gilbert's knights. Forced to kill several of them in self-defense, Hereward and Martin leave Gilbert's household and move to Cornwall, where Hereward kills a crude ruffian named Ironhook, thereby saving a Cornish princess from an unhappy marriage. Through his heroic venture, the idea of chivalry, of assisting the weak, of keeping faith and honor, takes root in his heart. Following the killing of Ironhook, Hereward and Martin appear, for a brief space, in the service of the Viking King Ranald Sigtrygsson. In Ranald's service, Hereward proves himself as adept with harp and song as with his sword Brainbiter. He makes a lifelong friend of the young prince Sigtryg when he assists the prince in rescuing the Cornish princess from yet another unwanted marriage and delivering her to Sigtryg.

From the court of Ranald on the coast of Ireland, Hereward and his retinue sail to the Continent, where they join the court of Baldwin of Flanders. As members of the court, they assist Baldwin against the Count of Guisnes. Hereward and his Vikings are amused by what passes for warfare between the two sides:

. . . there was the usual splintering of lances and slipping up of horses, and hewing at heads and shoulders so well defended in mail that no one was much hurt. The archers and arbalisters, meanwhile, amused themselves by shooting at the castle walls, out of which they chipped several small pieces of stone. And when they were all tired, they drew off on both sides, and went in to dinner. (XI, p. 132)

On the next day, Hereward asks permission to fight the knights of

Guisnes. Contemptuous of the "footpad churls," the knights ride at the Vikings, who chop off the horses' heads. Proclaiming that he came to fight, not to joust, Hereward retires until the next day. Then he singles out a particularly splendid knight, the nephew of the Count of Guisnes, knocks him senseless, and, under the gaze of the other knights, carries him bodily from the field. The war ends abruptly. Hereward's fame returns to St. Omer before him and attracts the attention of the lady Torfrida, who sets out to win him. As keen in a tournament as on the battlefield, Hereward wins Torfrida by defeating a rival suitor. As a pledge of her love, Torfrida gives Hereward a suit of magic armor, making him impregnable to his enemies. Torfrida's only regret is that although Hereward is courageous, he lacks polish. Consequently, she educates him, setting before him the example of the ancient heroes. He learns from her what he would have rejected from another source, demonstrating again that woman's tact and purity are the only spell that can civilize man.

Not many months after Hereward and Torfrida are married, Hereward is swept up by events that change the direction of his life. In 1066, Hereward, who believes Swegn of Denmark should be king of England, watches helplessly as invading armies prepare for their English campaign. England is besieged by two contending forces. The first is eliminated by the death of the leader Harold Hardraade. The second, led by William of Normandy, succeeds when the English King Harold is killed at the Battle of Hastings. William then begins systematically to subdue the English to Norman rule.

Refugees convince Hereward that England is in bad straits and that only he can save the country from the Normans. He and Martin go to England in disguise and find that although many are determined to resist the Normans, none of the English has enough stature to unite the people. When he discovers that the Normans have killed his young brother and driven his mother from her home, Hereward butchers the usurpers of his mother's estate, sends his mother to Crowland Abbey, and vows to fight as long as a Frenchman lives in England. Following these deeds and Hereward's subsequent knighting by the English church, the Normans send word to Ivo Taillesbois and to William, informing them of Hereward's return.

Bringing Torfrida and their young daughter to England, Hereward and his army settle in the fens, where they are left alone by

William, who continues his systematic conquest of the country. By
the winter of 1070–1071, William has confined Hereward without
having to fight him, and Hereward's confidence wanes. Yet
Torfrida urges him to struggle on, winning glory through defiance.

When an attempt by Swegn of Denmark fails to unseat the
Normans, Swegn offers Hereward and his other English supporters
refuge in Denmark; however, Hereward refuses, preferring to die
in England. As the Danes withdraw, the Normans march on Ely,
trapping Hereward and his retinue. Unable to capture it, the
Normans withdraw. They track Hereward to his fenland lair, however, and are repulsed again and again by Hereward and his men
who, inspired by Torfrida, wound William and set fire to the fens,
slaughtering the Normans. Although the English win the battle,
Hereward realizes his cause is doomed and begins to dream of
making the best peace he can for the sake of his men and then of
dying at sea or in Danish exile.

Hereward's cause is not helped by the monks of Ely, who make a
separate peace with the Normans, nor by various of his supporters
who desert him. In retreat, Hereward and his army move to the
greenwood, where they live as outlaws. From their forest refuge,
they raid the French holders of what was originally their own land.
In the greenwood, Hereward receives a letter from Alftruda, who is
now grown and eager to seduce him, warning him that forces are
being raised against him and suggesting that he capitulate and
pledge his allegiance to William. The letter awakens memories of
better, more heroic times, and Hereward begins to yearn for
Alftruda.

Meanwhile, life in the forest exhausts Hereward and Torfrida.
They grow cold toward each other until finally an unbridgeable
gulf appears between them. Torfrida discovers a letter from
Alftruda congratulating Hereward on his freedom from his wife
and promising marriage to herself if he will come to William. In
despair, Torfrida joins Hereward's mother at Crowland Abbey,
and Hereward returns the magic armor. With the loss of Torfrida,
Hereward declines rapidly. He picks a quarrel with an unknown
Englishman, and, in a fight which ends in a draw, breaks his sword
Brainbiter. Then he violates his own principles by making peace
with William and marrying Alftruda. But Hereward's enemies
among the Normans give him no peace. In particular Ivo
Taillesbois swears to kill Hereward. Hereward himself is bitter;
gnawed by consciousness of his shame, he sinks back into the vices

from which Torfrida had raised him years before.

One day in 1075 Hereward, seated in his ancestral home with an old Viking comrade named Winter, is surprised by Ivo Taillesbois and a band of treacherous knights, which includes Hereward's Norman son-in-law. For a few moments, Hereward and Winter recover their youthful strength. As Hereward fights, he thinks of Torfrida and as he falls he cries her name. After Hereward's death, Torfrida and Martin claim Hereward's body and remove his head from the gable of his ancestral hall. Austere and commanding in her bearing, Torfrida shrivels the traitorous knights with a glance and intimidates Alftruda into surrendering Hereward's body. Returning to Crowland, she buries Hereward and years later is buried with him in his grave.

The novel ends with Hereward and Torfrida's granddaughter and her husband, now elderly themselves, planning to decorate the family tomb. They have lived well, for if Hereward and Torfrida were the last of the old English, daring in war, their granddaughter and her husband are the first of the new English. Daring to be peaceful, they drained the fens and made the nation prosper.

Like *Hypatia* and *Westward Ho!*, *Hereward the Wake*, Kingsley's last novel, focuses on an historically critical event. In *Hypatia* it was the fall of the Roman empire; in *Westward Ho!* it was the Spanish crisis of 1588, from which England emerged as a world power. *Hereward the Wake*, as bloodthirsty a novel as *Westward Ho!*, focuses on the Norman Conquest and on the efforts of the last English hero to resist it. It portrays, in effect, the death of old England and the birth of the new.

Unlike *Hypatia* and *Westward Ho!*, *Hereward the Wake* is a straightforward heroic narrative. The episodes are arranged chronologically to show Hereward's rise and fall and to emphasize the central theme: physical strength unsupported by an ameliorative principle is not enough to sustain a hero. In order to present the story of Hereward and Torfrida, however, Kingsley was forced to treat the subject of marital infidelity, a topic with which he could not have been comfortable had the story not been set so far in the past. Placing this topic, disturbing to most Victorians, in a novel set in the eleventh century, enabled Kingsley to treat it from a distance and to reinforce for his immediate audience the central theme established by his episodic arrangement of the plot. In addition to simplifying his narrative structure by eliminating complicated sub-

plots, Kingsley, in *Hereward the Wake,* both reduced the number
of his characters and simplified the nature of all of them except
Hereward and Torfrida.

Hereward is a Viking and as such identifies himself with
Germanic heroes such as Beowulf. Although he values physical
strength and prowess in battle, he is equally skilled at singing heroic
songs to the accompaniment of a harp. He is concerned with reputation and, at least as a young man, accepts battle as a way of
proving his manhood and of earning the sobriquet "the Wake" by
being alert to danger.

In developing Hereward's character, Kingsley broke with the
pattern of his earlier novels by not providing his hero with an antagonist whose role clarifies by contrast. Moreover, from episode
to episode, Hereward is accompanied by Vikings, but none of them
is developed as his foil. From episode to episode, Hereward meets
and is either admired by young men such as Arnoul, who wishes to
become a Viking, or is challenged by drunken bullies such as
Ironhook. Although the plot presents a number of potential foils
and antagonists, none of them is sufficiently developed to serve as
such.

Once Hereward's character has been established and his career is
underway, the logical choice for antagonist is William the Conqueror. Kingsley states, however, that his sources do not present a
clear picture of William, and, as a result, the Conqueror's portrait
remains shadowy. In place of this worthy antagonist, Kingsley
presents Ivo Taillesbois, a crude butcher without the greatness of
William in this novel or the complexity of Don Guzman in *Westward Ho!* Hereward remains a hero without a peer and therefore if
one seeks a fitting antagonist for him, one must look within
Hereward himself.

Hereward is the best example among Kingsley's heroes of what
Masao Miyoshi[33] and others have called "the divided self." The
better part of Hereward seeks to do his duty, to protect the weak,
and possibly to drive William from England. Another part of Hereward, like the mariners in Tennyson's "The Lotus-Eaters," tires of
the never-ending struggle and seeks to make a separate peace. This
tension, central to Hereward's character, is portrayed through the
influence upon him of the two women in his life.

As is clear from Kingsley's female characters in his earlier novels,
their function is to civilize men and to inspire them to attain the
best that is in them; they are, in short, the biblical "helpmate." It is

the Brotherhood of the Rose in *Westward Ho!* which organizes youthful Elizabethan men to export English civilization to the New World. In *Two Years Ago* it is Valentia St. Just who inspires Frank Headley to become the leading parson of Aberalva; it is Grace Harvey to whom the sadder but wiser Tom Thurnall returns from the Crimea in search of moral guidance; and it is the rejection of his wife which dooms Elsley Vavasour.

In *Hereward the Wake,* Torfrida's importance is enhanced by her husband's weakness. In Flanders, Torfrida tames, educates, and ennobles her rough English lover. Before their marriage, Hereward tells Torfrida,

"Ah! we are rough wooers, we sea rovers. We cannot pay glozing French compliments like your knights here, who fawn on a damsel with soft words in the hall, will kiss the dust off their queen's feet, and die for a hair of their goddess's eyebrow .... We are rough, lady, we English: but those who trust us find us true." (XI, p. 159)

Married to Hereward, Torfrida is embarrassed by these rough English ways. Consequently, she teaches him and trains him to bear himself as a knight. She lectures him on "chivalry," "self-sacrifice," "respect to the weak," and "devotion to God" (XI, p. 169). Torfrida calls upon the example of the ancient heroes and the martyrs, and finally, the lessons take:

... the spell was on him — a far surer, as well as purer spell than any love-potion of which foolish Torfrida had ever dreamed — the only spell which can really civilise man — that of a woman's tact, and woman's purity. (XI, p. 169)

Although Hereward occasionally lapses into drunkenness, his rough edges are smoothed by Torfrida, and his energy is given direction and purpose by his marriage. Torfrida and their daughter become for Hereward the "home" and "family" for whom a man does his "duty." As long as life proceeds with its usual round of Continental wars and intervals of peace, Hereward's strength is sufficient. In Flanders, therefore, Torfrida's wifely ministrations fulfill the requirements of a Kingsley heroine in the usual ways.

Hereward's weakness becomes apparent not in Flanders, but in England, and as it does, Torfrida's own courage and savage dignity become clear, making her in some ways the most attractive of Kingsley's heroines. Leaving Flanders for England, Torfrida adopts Hereward's cause as her own. She addresses the troops on her arrival, instructs them on the building of fortifications, suggests tactics to Hereward, and inspires the army by being present at critical battles. As Hereward's eventual defeat becomes sure, his faith in himself and his ideals wanes, and he yearns for peace and for Alftruda.

When the English are apparently trapped at Aldreth and Hereward fears destruction, he considers abandoning his army:

Was it worth while to fight, to die, for them, for anything? What was William to him? What was England? Why play out the lost game to the last? Why not leave all behind, and ride down south — to the sea — the free sea, and the wild joys of the Viking's life? (XII, p. 115)

But the memory of Torfrida and his daughter recalls him from his reverie and he returns to them and his duty in the fens. Again Hereward despairs. He has heard witches prophesy his defeat. Torfrida counters Hereward's despair by suggesting that he ignite the fens and thereby entrap William's men in flames. As the battle approaches, Torfrida works herself into a religious frenzy and, prophesying the destruction of the French, dresses in sackcloth and chains and rides on a white charger at the head of the English army. The English defeat the French.

However determined Torfrida's purpose is before Hereward's weakness destroys him, her savage dignity is nowhere more apparent than in Chapter 41, "How Hereward Began to Get His Soul's Price." Unlike Hereward, Torfrida is never beaten. Three days after the murder of Hereward, Torfrida comes among his murderers to claim his body. She is dressed in black, her hair is white, and she is thin and sharp-featured with hawk-like eyes. She speaks "slowly and quietly, but with an intensity . . . more terrible than rage" (XII, p. 251). She fixes on each man in turn her "terrible eyes"; each murderer hangs his head like a "rated cur" (XII, p. 252). Meeting Alftruda, who is tending Hereward's body, Torfrida fixes her with her eyes and sends her shrieking from the room. Torfrida returns to Crowland, where she buries Hereward and prays that he find peace. When she dies, she is buried in Hereward's tomb. Torfrida's dignity, won against adversity as she confronts her fate in an alien land, makes her majestic and sets her apart from Kingsley's other heroines.

Torfrida pulls Hereward toward adherence to duty and principle;

Alftruda pulls him toward faithlessness and betrayal of his ideals. Thus, if Hereward lacks an opposite, Torfrida does not. Alftruda is vain, covetous, deceitful, and self-centered from the moment she first appears. Her deceit in love combines with William's cunning in war to unman and defeat Hereward. She lusts for marriage to Hereward, but she possesses neither the substance nor the will to sustain him. She begs compromise and surrender where Torfrida supports resistance and adherence to principles. Alftruda appeals to Hereward at the end of his career by being a reminder of its beginning, of that period when as an heroic youth he had saved her from the polar bear. She appeals to him when he has tired of the war with William and when he realizes that he cannot win. She promises him marriage to herself, still young and beautiful, and honors from William if Hereward will make his peace. In brief, Alftruda promises Hereward what Tennyson's portrayal of Lotus Land promises Ulysses's mariners: rest from toil and a life of ease.

Neither Hereward nor Alftruda is made happy by the match. Although he is "besotted" by Alftruda, Hereward loves Torfrida and is gnawed by guilt and convinced that his comrades despise him. Conscious of evil and aware that he has chosen it, Hereward descends into the drunkenness and coarseness from which Torfrida had raised him. Alftruda becomes a shrew, berating Hereward for loving his first wife better than herself, and, lacking the power to raise him from his degradation, she becomes disgusted by him. Hereward's sin "was not punished by miracle. What sin is? It worked out its own punishment; that which it merited, deserved, or earned, by its own labour" (XII, p. 241).

Although Kingsley developed Hereward and Torfrida fully, he greatly simplified the secondary characters in *Hereward the Wake*. Lady Godiva, Hereward's mother, is a religious fanatic whose saintliness places her under the control of unscrupulous monks and causes her to outlaw Hereward. Although she is therefore necessary to the plot,[34] she does not grow. Abbot Brand is a monk to Kingsley's liking: he is stern and disciplined, but he is also kind, offering aid to Hereward when he is newly outlawed. Furthermore, not opposed to handling a spear himself, Abbot Brand possesses the devotion of a monk and the courage of a knight and can therefore be considered a "muscular Christian."[35] Martin Lightfoot is loyal, bold, courageous, revengeful, and grotesque. He acts as a jester and as a guardian for the wilder Hereward, and he is the source of what humor there is in the novel.

The plot and characterization of *Hereward the Wake* are less complicated than are their counterparts in Kingsley's other novels. The straightforward, episodic plot and the reduced number of important characters focus attention on the rise and fall of the hero as he learns the lesson Kingsley wishes to teach: physical strength unsupported by an ameliorative principle is incapable of sustaining a hero. It is to Kingsley's credit as a novelist that although the didacticism of the story may no longer appeal, the portraits of Hereward and Torfrida and the story of their unhappy fate still do.

Hypatia, Westward Ho!, and *Hereward the Wake* portray three crises in world history, in each of which Kingsley believed God had made His will manifest. *Yeast, Alton Locke,* and *Two Years Ago* present nineteenth-century crises in which Kingsley believed he saw God at work. The three historical novels complete Kingsley's providential vision by showing the crises of his own age to be best understood as evidence that God is active in the modern world.

CHAPTER 6

Poetry and Prose Idylls

I *Poetry*

CHARLES Kingsley wrote his last poem, "Lorraine, Lorraine, Lorrèe," in Colorado in June 1874. The writing of poetry was, however, important to Kingsley throughout his literary career, not just at the end of it. By 1852, the writing of poetry had become so attractive that he considered giving up fiction for its sake. At work on *Phaeton* and *Hypatia,* Kingsley announced to J. M. Ludlow his resolution to write no more novels: "I will write poetry — not as a profession — but I will keep myself for it, and I do think I shall do something that will live."[1]

Also by 1852 Kingsley had attempted to reinterest his publisher John Parker in producing a volume of his poems. Parker, however, remained unmoved until 1857, when he agreed, probably because an American edition, culled from periodicals and published by Ticknor and Fields, had appeared in 1856.[2] Parker's edition of Kingsley's *Andromeda and Other Poems* appeared in 1858; in 1872, Macmillan published a collected edition titled *Poems; Including The Saint's Tragedy, Andromeda, Songs, Ballads, etc.*[3] When his poems appeared in 1858, Kingsley thought them overrated:

. . . I know I can put into singing words the plain things I see and feel; but . . . — the power of metaphor and analogue — the instructive vision of connections between things in heaven and earth, which poets *must* have is very weak in me; and therefore I shall never be a great poet.[4]

Nevertheless, Kingsley believed "my poetry is all of me which will last," but felt compelled to add "Except, perhaps, 'Hypatia.'"[5]

Kingsley's determination to "do what I can"[6] in poetry, recognizing his limitations, produced a respectable body of poems, the best of which are songs and ballads. Kingsley's poetic practice follows from his belief that without faith there can be no real art, for art is the outward expression of firm, coherent belief. And a poetry of doubt, even a sceptical poetry, in its true sense, can never possess clear and sound form, even organic form at all.[7]

In Kingsley's view, the absence of "firm coherent belief," which would provide a "uniting idea," caused the poets of the nineteenth century to be "altogether fragmentary" and to produce a "'poetry of doubt,' [which] however pretty would stand us in little stead if we were threatened with a second Armada." What is needed is a poet who will "sing about things which concern all men, in language which all men can understand."[8]

Kingsley's poetic credo is clarified by his judgments on the poetry of his age. Finding that the modern poetry which causes German hearts to leap is characterized by "simplicity, manhood, clearness, finished melody," Kingsley turns to modern British poetry. Not surprisingly, he finds that

the modern poetry which lives on the lips and in the hearts of Englishmen, Scotchmen, Irishmen . . . is not only simple in form and language, but much of it [is] fitted . . . to tunes already existing.[9]

Thus, Kingsley praises Burns's "Scots Wha Ha' Wi' Wallace Bled," Moore's "Let Erin Remember the Days of Old," Campbell's "Mariners of England" and "Rule Britannia," and Hood's "Song of the Shirt."[10]

Kingsley's own best poems are fashioned in this mode: that is, they are songs and ballads, poems characterized by "simplicity," "clearness," "finished melody," and established form. They are also frequently didactic. Kingsley's least satisfying poems are also his most ambitious: "Andromeda" (1852) and "Saint Maura: A.D. 304" (1852).

As Una Pope-Hennessey has observed, both "Andromeda" and "Saint Maura" deal with the martyrdom of a woman, one of Kingsley's favorite themes. "Andromeda," a retelling of Perseus's rescue of Andromeda, is the more deliberately artful of the two, for with it Kingsley attempted not only to write on a subject which engaged him deeply but also to reinstate hexameters, "that king of meters," in the English tongue.[11] At least one near contemporary, Frederick Harrison, believed "Andromeda" almost to have succeeded in reviving English hexameters. He judged some five hundred lines to be among the best poetry in the language in rhythm, ease, rapidity, and metrical correctness.[12] Another, Lafcadio Hearn, agreed, stating that Kingsley is the best writer of hexameters in the English language.[13] One of Kingsley's twentieth-century biographers, R. B. Martin, echoes Hearn's judgment, pointing out that Kingsley's best use of the meter appears in those sections which move "away from characterization of nature."[14] As Martin also points out, Kingsley was not the only Victorian to be attracted to the Andromeda myth, for John Bell had displayed a bronze statue of Andromeda at the Great Exhibition. Furthermore, Robert Browning employed the story as the central motif in *The Ring and the Book,* dedicating his poem to the memory of Elizabeth Barrett Browning, just as Kingsley had earlier written "Andromeda" for his own wife, Fanny. Each poet, like the age in general, seems to have found in the story of Perseus's rescue of Andromeda from a sea monster an analogy to the problems of courtship in the face of family disapproval.[15]

Kingsley's other long, ambitious poem, "Saint Maura, A.D. 304," is a blank-verse dramatic monologue on the subject of marriage and salvation. It is delivered by a naked, pregnant woman to her blinded husband after both have been tortured and crucified for refusing to worship false gods. Kingsley himself told J. M. Ludlow the poem was "the deepest and clearest thing I have yet done."[16] and he reported to F. D. Maurice that nothing he had ever written had caused him such "a poetic fervour."[17] Nevertheless, Kingsley's enthusiasm was not shared by his contemporaries, *Fraser's* reviewer finding it an "unhealthy" poem and the reader for the *Saturday Review* judging it to be horrible, though of undeniable power.[18] Modern readers find it morbid,[19] even prurient, in its savoring of wounds and whippings.

Kingsley's shorter, less ambitious poems are of several kinds. He wrote occasional poems, both serious and comic. Among the serious are "Ode on the Installation of the Duke of Devonshire, Chancellor of the University of Cambridge, 1862"; and "Easter Week" (1867), written for the opening of a new wing of the Children's Hospital, Birmingham. The comic occasional poems are invitations to either or both Tom Hughes and J. A. Froude to join him on a fishing trip, usually in Wales. These poems, "The Invitation: To Tom Hughes" (1856), "Fishing Song: To J. A. Froude and Tom Hughes" (1856), and "Pen-Y-Gwrydd: To Tom Hughes" (1857), reveal a playful side of Kingsley's character not often apparent in his other work. Still another of his occasional poems, "On the Death of a Certain Journal" (1852) (published as "Epicedium" in the *Christian Socialist*) bitterly laments the end of the *Christian Socialist* as having been caused by "the bigot's curse,/The pedant's frown, the worldling's yawn." Among these occasional poems, then, are a formal ode, lofty in subject and puffy in treatment; a song and a hymn, both set to music; witty invitations, as colloquial in manner as playful in spirit; and a bitter expression of social conscience.

As is evident, Kingsley valued poems characterized by simplicity, "clearness," "finished melody," and established form. Ballads and brief lyrics were therefore suited both to his taste and to his talent. The ballad, unmarked by arresting figures of speech or novel turns of phrase, simple in setting and characterization, and focused on a single dramatic incident, appealed to him. So too did the brief lyric, which concentrated on a single deeply felt emotion. The requirements of these forms, as Kingsley practiced them, imposed on his poetry a focus often missing in his novels.

Many of Kingsley's ballads imitate the poetic traditions of the fifteenth century and employ deliberately archaic language, much after the manner of Edmund Spenser, one of his favorite poets. "The Weird Lady" (1840), for example, deals with Earl Harold's captivity in the Weird Lady's "charmed castle over the sea," and with the death of the Earl's wife in "his own countrie." In "The Red King" (1847), Kingsley constructs a moral narrative which teaches that England will not house kings that "harrow Christian men." In an opening which echoes the ballad of Sir Patrick Spens, the cruel Red King is drinking in his hall when he is interrupted by a monk who comes to tell of "A grimly sweven I dreamt yestreen." The dream foretells the king's death, which occurs on schedule when the drunken king goes hunting with a knight "who smiled full grim that day" and, with a well-placed arrow, frees the country of its wastrel ruler. Kingsley's other ballads are on the same order. They concentrate on a single incident, often with social implications, antique the language, and tell the story.

Kingsley's interest in ballads was considerable; nevertheless, he also wrote a sizable number of brief lyrics which develop themes that appear most notably and elaborately in his novels. Of the three principal themes which appear in these lyrics, one asserts that God's unaging spirit keeps the world young. Another declaims against social wrongs and agitates for reform. The third praises physical exertion and heroism, the "muscularity" of muscular Christianity.

Poems developing the theme that, despite appearances, the world is young characteristically assert the presence of God's spirit in nature, a presence testified to by green leaves and spring blossoms. Among the poems which develop this theme are "A Parable from Liebig" (1848), "Old and New: A Parable" (1848), and "The World's Age" (1849).

In "A Parable from Liebig," the devil sits on a rotting tree stump, rejoicing that faith has grown cold as the winter. His joy is dashed, however, when a spirit crumbles the stump and announces,

> "Yon wood does but perish new seedlings to cherish,
> And the world is too live yet for thee."

The first stanza of "Old and New: A Parable," observes that nothing endures. But the second of the two stanzas reverses the judgment:

> . . . see the spring-blossoms steal forth a-maying,
> Clothing with tender hues orchard and glen;
> So, though old forms pass by, ne'er shall their spirit die,
> Look! England's bare boughs show green leaf again.

In "The World's Age," Kingsley gives the theme a social turn. First, he finds the worn-out condition of society to be evidence of the world's age and then asserts that, despite appearances, the spirit of heroism survives. To those who believe the world is dying, Kingsley exclaims his assurance that

> Sparks from Heaven, within us lying,
> Flash, and will flash till the last.

Despite social conditions that make the earth appear an anteroom to hell

> Still the race of Hero-spirits
>   Pass the lamp from hand to hand;
> . . . .
> Still the youthful hunter gathers
>   Fiery joy from wold and wood;
> He will dare as dared his fathers
>   Give him cause as good.

God's spirit, akin here to the spirit of heroism, will yet flash out
and prove its reality just as surely as the spirit in "A Parable from
Liebig" crumbled the rotting stump on which the devil sat.

However interesting these poems may be for thematic reasons,
Kingsley's most successful lyrics are "Dartside" (1849) and two
songs from *The Water-Babies:* "The Tide River" (1862) and "The
Summer Sea" (1862). In "Dartside," the speaker remarks that although he is unable to interpret exactly what nature says, he is con-
fident that a spirit dwells there and that one day he will understand
the message:

> I cannot tell what you say, green leaves,
>   I cannot tell what you say:
> But I know that there is a spirit in you,
>   And a word in you this day.

In "The Tide River," the river speaks, tracing its route from its
undefiled country origin, past the fetid city sewers, to the strong,
free ocean and the golden sands along the shore. Where it is clean,
the river invites mother and child to bathe; where it is polluted by
the city's filth, it warns mother and child away. Finally, the river
traces in its flow from cleanliness through defilement to cleanliness
an analogue to the progress of the human soul:

> Strong and free, strong and free;
>   The floodgates are open, away to the sea.
> Free and strong, free and strong,
>   Cleansing my streams as I hurry along
> To the golden sands, and the leaping bar,
> And the taintless tide that awaits me afar,
> As I lose myself in the infinite main,
> Like a soul that has sinned and is pardoned again.
>   Undefiled, for the undefiled;
> Play by me, bathe in me, mother and child.

"The Summer Sea," sung in *The Water-Babies* by a young mother
with a child in her arms, is a prayer to the "soft, soft wind" and to
the love of God to cool and bless her and her child:

> Soft soft wind, from out the sweet south sliding
> Waft thy silver cloud-webs athwart the summer sea;
>   Thin thin threads of mist on dewy fingers twining
> Weave a veil of dappled gauze to shade my babe and me.

Deep deep Love, within thy own abyss abiding,
Pour Thyself abroad, O Lord, on earth and air and sea;
Worn weary hearts within Thy holy temple hiding.
Shield from sorrow, sin, and shame my helpless babe and me.

The movement of these three poems exhibits a finer touch and manages better than do most of the others a delicacy of language within Kingsley's required simplicity of form.

Among poems of a more revolutionary spirit, in addition to "On the Death of a Certain Journal," "The Red King," and "The World's Age" noted above, are "The Bad Squire" (1847) from *Yeast,* "Weep, Weep, Weep, and Weep" (1849) from *Alton Locke,* and "A Thought from the Rhine" (1851). Each poem deals with the plight of the working classes and suggests, in its own way, that a day of reckoning is inevitable.

The last thematic group to be mentioned praises physical exertion and heroism. "My Hunting Song" (1849) and "The Delectable Day' (1872) both exalt hard riding and vigorous living:

Forward! Hark forward's the cry!
One more fence and we're out on the open,
So to us at once, if you want to live near us!

Rollicking lines and a hearty halloo characterize these poems, which find their heroic apotheosis in "The Longbeards' Saga, A.D. 400" (1852) from *Hypatia* and "Ode to the North-East Wind" (1854). In "The Longbeards' Saga," Teutonic heroes who have been living too softly in Alexandria recall their homeland and the lively swordplay which is their proper sport. In language reminiscent of Old English verse techniques, the Teutons sing with a grim joy:

"Who are these heroes tall, —
Lusty-limbed Longbeards?
Over the swans' bath
Why cry they to me?
Bones should be crashing fast,
Wolves should be full-fed,
Where such, mad-hearted,
Swing hands in the sword-play."

In "Ode to the North-East Wind," Kingsley scorns a milder zephyr as "the ladies' breeze" and celebrates the harsh northeast wind for building "hard English men." It is this wind that drives "English hearts of oak/ Seaward round the world." Kingsley closes the ode with a prayer to the wind to stir England's "Vikings' blood" and to brace the "brain and sinew" of Englishmen.

From ballads, odes, and soft, delicate songs, through poems bristling with indignation at social injustice, to the celebration of the heroic spirit, Kingsley was concerned to turn his limited poetic talents to the service of his ideals. In poems of established form, characterized by simplicity, "clearness," and "finished melody," he wrote of a living, not a mechanical nature, of a divine spirit pervading and perennially renewing life, and advocated the heroic attitude which he believed would revitalize English life and bring on another Golden Age. These themes and this attitude he returned to again and again in his poetry and elaborated in his novels.

II *Prose Idylls*

Most readers today are familiar with the idyll, if at all, through its association with Tennyson's *Idylls of the King.* Yet the idyll is an ancient form whose classical antecedents are to be found in the works of Theocritus and Bion. Never a rigid form, the idyll, either a poem or a short prose composition, characteristically treats pastoral subjects, incorporating beautiful rural scenery as a necessary ingredient, and portrays a life of innocence and tranquility. Kingsley's idylls, first published in periodicals and later collected and published as *Prose Idylls, New and Old* (1873), fulfill the few requirements of the form. Moreover, the scene, in Kingsley's hands, provides the occasion for moral reflection on favorite themes.

The topics are as various and as numerous as the issues and ideas of mid-Victorian England itself. Among the most frequently recurring, however, are "minute philosophy" and the idea of progress. Kingsley's advocacy of what he termed "minute philosophy" is of particular importance to our understanding of the idylls, for it establishes fundamental relationships between man and nature and between man, nature, and God essential to our understanding of Kingsley's position regarding progress and art.

The central idea of minute philosophy is that a close examination of one's immediate surroundings will yield a microcosm of the universe. One need not travel far afield to learn the truths of God and man: they are available in fifteen miles of moorland or in a small section of an English chalk stream. In "North Devon: Exmoor" (1849), Kingsley asserts that the student of the small local scene discovers sooner than those whose subjects may be grander, the "'power of discovering the infinite in the finite'" (XVIII, p. 156) and of finding in trivial phenomena their true relation to the whole of the universe. In "North Devon: the Coast-Line" (1849), the artist Claude Mellot returns to the narrator and regrets that the scene has been too magnificent to reduce to canvas and that painting anything beyond a frond of fern would frustrate him. The narrator reminds him that "The little infinite in them would have baffled you just as much as the only somewhat bigger infinite of the hills on which they grow" (XVIII, p. 156). In "My Winter Garden" (1858), Kingsley creates a narrator who justifies his life to an old friend who has been living in India. As a young man, the narrator had wanted to travel, but had been unable to; consequently, he examined what he found at hand, discovering that if we have eyes to see it the infinite miracle of nature exists in every tuft of grass. In "Chalk-Stream Studies" (1858), the fisherman finds in the streams close at hand sufficient challenge to warrant his effort as well as knowledge of the "inside" of the country.

Kingsley's explication of minute philosophy is central to understanding his attitudes toward science and toward the idea of progress. In the idylls, Kingsley's descriptive passages and his references to books and articles on various geological and biological subjects testify to both his own close observation of nature and to the breadth of his reading on scientific subjects. What is at stake here is, nevertheless, Kingsley's belief that closely observing nature not only enables one to discover the evolutionary process but also imposes on him the duty of directing that process, and thereby fulfilling his role in creation.

Charles Kingsley shared with many other mid-Victorians a belief in progress and the optimism that the cultivation of science would enable mankind to advance more rapidly and more certainly than ever before. Evolutionary theories, particularly Darwin's, made possible the reading of the evidence of paleontology as a record of progressive development. Progress seemed to be a world-process, a law of the universe.[20] If Kingsley welcomed the Darwinian hypothesis, he also welcomed the possibility that discovering the dynamic laws of historical progress, the cause and effect relationships between men and events, would enable man to develop the means of accelerating natural progress wherever it was beneficial and to compensate for its lapses elsewhere. Kingsley, like Thomas Huxley, looked forward to the day when society might be reconstructed on a scientific basis,[21] "when Sanitary Reform and Social Science shall be accepted and carried out as primary duties of a government toward the nation" (XVIII, p. 195). Thus, the *Prose Idylls* are everywhere filled with geological and biological observations which, in addition to pointing out the value of minute philosophy, more importantly assert the value of using science to subdue nature to the service of mankind.

Kingsley's lengthy reflections on time in "North Devon" and his description of evolutionary process there and in "The Fens" (1873) identify progress, the law of the universe, with the spirit of God and assert that although material nature may change, the spirit of God is constant. The close observation of nature is therefore a fundamentally sacred obligation, for it puts mankind into communication with the only true reality: the spirit of God. In "From Ocean to Sea" (1873), Kingsley identifies the progress of mankind as progress from barbarism to civilization, but in the earlier "North Devon: Clovelly" (1849), he summarizes this development and projects its continuation into the future:

Gone they all are, Cymry and Roman, Saxon and Norman; and upon the ruins of their accumulated labour we stand here. Each of them had his use, — planted a few more trees or cleared a few more, tilled a fresh scrap of down, organized a scrap more of chaos. Who dare wish the tide of improvement, which has been flowing for nineteen centuries, swifter and swifter still as it goes on, to stop, just because it is not convenient to us just now to move on? It will not take another nineteen hundred years, be sure, to make even this lovely nook as superior to what it is now to the little knot of fishing huts where naked Britons peeped out, trembling at the iron tramp of each insolent legionary from the camp above. (XVIII, p. 191)

In this quotation resides Kingsley's and the mid-Victorian's vision: each successive generation from the beginning of time, carried by the inexorable "tide of improvement," building on the foundations of the one before, organizing a bit more of "chaos," and leading to a future certain to be superior to the trembling present. It suggests a view of the mid-Victorian, for all of his certainties, caught in the present moment between past and future, a transitional being upon whose efforts the next generation depends. It is a vision at once optimistic and obligatory.

The principal obligation which Kingsley discusses in the idylls is that of continuing to conquer and subdue nature, in other words to continue the process described in the preceding quotation of organizing "a scrap more of chaos." The idea that it is man's duty to conquer and subdue nature appears in several of the idylls; however, it appears most prominently in "Chalk-Stream Studies," "The Fens," and "North Devon: Morte" (1849).

In "Chalk-Stream Studies," the fulfillment of the duty to conquer and subdue overcomes one's "sense of waste and incompleteness in all scenery where man has not fulfilled the commission of Eden, 'to dress it and to keep it'" (XVIII, p. 24). In "The Fens," Kingsley celebrates the improvement of life and the increase of arable land caused by the draining of the fens. Describing the struggle of the fen-dwellers against the fens in the heroic language he employed in describing the exploits of Teutonic warriors *(Two Years Ago),* Amyas Leigh *(Westward Ho!)* and Hereward *(Hereward the Wake),* Kingsley celebrates the draining of the fens first by windmills and then by steam-engines. The fens were "subdued" and man's lot made more prosperous by heroic English persistence in an 800-year-old struggle with the sea and by nineteenth-century technology:

. . . instead of mammoth and urus, stag and goat, that fen feeds cattle many times more numerous than all the wild venison of the primaeval jungle; and produces crops capable of nourishing a hundred times as many human beings; and more — it produces men a hundred times as numerous as ever it produced before; more healthy and long-lived — and if they will, more virtuous and more happy — than was ever Girvian in his log-canoe, or holy hermit in his cell. (XVIII, p. 90)

For Kingsley, in spite of his appreciation of the beauty of untamed nature, wherever the cultivated garden conflicts with the romantic wilderness, the garden wins. The conclusion of this idyll corresponds to the conclusion of *Hereward the Wake,* itself set in the fens, in which Hereward's descendants are shown to be successful fen-dwellers, the heroes of the future, who have traded swords for plows.

But it is in the earlier "North Devon: Morte," that as Kingsley hymns his praise to the railroad, his vision becomes most revealing:

. . . the new motion of our age — the rush of the express-train, when the live iron pants and leaps and roars through the long chalk cutting; and white mounds gleam cold a moment against the sky and vanish; and rocks, and grass, and bushes, fleet by in dim blended lines; and the long hedges revolve like the spokes of a gigantic wheel; and far below, meadows, and streams, and homesteads, with all their lazy old-world life, open for an instant, and then flee away; while awe-struck, silent, choked with the mingled sense of pride and helplessness, we are swept on by that great pulse of England's life-blood, rushing down her iron veins; and dimly out of the future looms the fulfillment of our primaeval mission, to conquer and subdue the earth, and space too, and time, and all things, — even, hardest of all tasks, yourselves, my cunning brothers . . . . (XVIII, p. 187)

The steam-engine applied to pumps drains the fens; applied to wheels it conquers time and space. It creates the force which propels the nineteenth century, enabling man to quicken the rate of progress — "for as swiftly rushes matter, more swiftly rushes mind" (XVIII, p. 187) — and yet, even for Kingsley, the steam-engine has its darker side. If Kingsley is awed to silence by the speed of the train, so is he silenced by the feeling of helplessness which overcomes him as he is hurtled toward the future which "looms" before him. The hardest task remains: man must yet subdue himself and learn the most difficult lesson of all, "that it is the Spirit of God which giveth you understanding" (XVIII, p. 187). This vision of mankind hurtling with increasing speed from the past into the future, a passenger propelled by a force which fills him with pride even as it increases his sense of helplessness, is peculiarly Victorian.[22]

Kingsley's belief that man's duty is to conquer and subdue the earth, to make a garden in the wilderness, finds its fictional expression primarily in *Westward Ho!* and in *Hereward the Wake*. The first novel justifies imperial expansion by taking the English to the New World, a world described in "North Devon: Lundy" (1849) as

the future world; the great Titan-baby, who will be teeming with new Athens and Londons . . . . Oh! when I look out here, like a bird from its cage, a captive from his dungeon, and remember what lies behind me, to what I must return to-morrow — the over-peopled Babylon of misery and misrule, puffery and covetousness — and there before me great countries untilled, uncivilized, unchristianized, crying aloud for man to come and be man indeed, and replenish the earth and subdue it. (XVIII, p. 208)

The second novel portrays, in its conclusion, the hero as farmer, a progress within the context of *Hereward the Wake* from admirable barbarism to an even more admirable agriculturalism.

The prose idyll is a form especially congenial to Kingsley's talent because it allowed him to exercise his descriptive powers and is at the same time loose enough in its requirements to permit, or encourage, digression and moral reflection on the issues of the day. Furthermore, the long descriptive passages in the novels, often landscape painting in prose, are reminiscent of his practice in the idylls. The lovingly detailed description of South American flora in *Westward Ho!* is, in fact, a prose idyll serving a novelistic purpose. Even more striking, however, is Kingsley's use in *Yeast* and *Alton Locke* of what might be called an "anti-idyll."

In "North Devon: Lundy," Kingsley's narrator explains to the painter Claude Mellot that Copley Fielding's South Down landscapes are "incomplete without a half-starved seven shillings a-week labourer in the foreground." His landscapes are "a text without a sermon . . . a premise without a conclusion" (XVIII, p. 205). In *Yeast* and *Alton Locke,* Kingsley strips the countryside of its romantic overlay and, by turning the pastoral meditation against itself, employs the technique of the idyll to highlight the poverty of farm laborers. In effect, he completes Copley Fielding's landscape by providing a sermon for the text.

CHAPTER 7

Conclusion

DURING his lifetime, Charles Kingsley was a leader in several of the important social movements of the mid-Victorian age and was consequently at the center of controversy. His literary work reflects the wide range of his interests and bears witness to the serious purposes which he hoped his art would serve. Today, looking back at nineteenth-century controversies and issues through Kingsley's fiction, poetry, and prose idylls more than 100 years after the immediate appeal of their topicality has disappeared, one may find himself agreeing with those critics who believe a study of Kingsley's life is more engaging than is a study of his literary work. Biographies of Kingsley continue to be published, and his literary work tends to be treated only insofar as it helps to elucidate his life and career. Because of this tendency to subordinate Kingsley's literary achievement to the ways it fits the context of his age, twentieth-century critics focus on Kingsley's didacticism or upon the propagandistic elements of his work.

This emphasis is, however, only partially correct. It is true that in our efforts to understand the Victorian age, we must see Kingsley's significance partly in his seeking "to make pastoral sense" out of a disordered and confusing period, in his attempt "to show the relevance of religion in helping men live their lives with some sort of personal stability, some hope, and at least some reconciliation to whatever is their fate."[1] But it is also true that the most appealing documents in which Kingsley made these attempts are literary. Any consideration of Kingsley's career must therefore close by stressing Kingsley not only as a man of his age but also as a writer of literature, for if it is true that Kingsley wrote literature with a purpose, it is also true that the impact of that literature is due not so much to its purpose as to its presentation.

In poetry, although Kingsley wrote several attractive lyrics and ballads, his voice is, admittedly, a minor one. The prose idyll allowed Kingsley to exploit his talent for writing descriptive prose, and in this genre he wrote pieces that have been undeservedly neglected. It is, however, the novel which made and sustains Kingsley's reputation. As a writer of fiction with a purpose, Kingsley has definite strengths which invite comparison with other Victorian authors such as Elizabeth Gaskell, Charles Dickens, Benjamin Disraeli, and Charlotte Brontë. Furthermore, as P. G. Scott points out in his excellent "Kingsley as Novelist," these strengths lie not in the propagandist element of Kingsley's fiction, but in his literary presentation of experience.[2]

Kingsley's condition of England novels — *Yeast, Alton Locke,* and *Two Years Ago* — are based upon his own observations, discussions with like-minded friends, and the reports of Parliamentary committees.[3] Kingsley was, in effect, popularizing more than discovering facts; what makes these novels important, therefore, is not their value as sociological documents but Kingsley's ability to infuse sociological observations with literary power. Each of Kingsley's condition of England novels is structured to reveal a number of contrasts between the rich and the poor, between England as it is and England as it might be, given sufficient vision. In each case, these contrasts work upon the mind of the central character to force his commitment to an ideal following a personal calamity: in *Yeast,* Lancelot, upon the loss of his fortune and the death of Argemone, dedicates his life to discovering a new social order founded on biblical precepts; in *Alton Locke,* Alton's vision of a new social order is clarified by a fever-ridden allegorical dream during a nearly fatal bout with typhus; in *Two Years Ago,* Tom returns to Grace Harvey chastened by imprisonment in the Crimea and receptive to Christianity. Through the structure Kingsley gives the lives of these central characters, he presents not sociological facts so much as his conception of earnest nineteenth-century Englishmen attempting to discover and live principled lives in a transitional age.

But as important as Kingsley's use of character in the condition of England novels is his ability to employ descriptive prose to achieve thematic and symbolic ends. In its portrayal of the conditions of the poor, Kingsley's prose often creates an horrific vision of hell on earth. *Alton Locke* provides one of the best examples:

It was a foul, chilly, foggy Saturday night. From the butchers' and greengrocers' shops the gas lights flared and flickered, wild and ghastly, over

haggard groups of slip-shod dirty women, bargaining for scraps of meat
and frost-bitten vegetables, wrangling about short weight and bad quality.
Fish-stalls and fruit stalls lined the edge of the greasy pavement, sending
up odours as foul as the language of sellers and buyers. Blood and sewer-
water crawled from under doors and out of spouts, and reeked down the
gutters among offal, animal and vegetable, in every stage of putrefaction.
Foul vapours rose from cowsheds and slaughter-houses, and the doorways
of undrained alleys, where the inhabitants carried the filth out on their
shoes from the backyard into the court, and from the court up into the
main street; while above, hanging like cliffs over the streets — those
narrow brawling torrents of filth, and poverty, and sin, — the houses with
their teeming load of life were piled up into the dingy, choking night. (VII,
p. 200)

Here, through his use of sensuously perceived details, Kingsley emphasizes the hellish scene: lamps "flare" and "flicker," the stench
of putrefying offal "reeks," sewer water oozes into the streets from
where it is carried into the homes of the teeming life, itself
described as a "load . . . piled up" like offal and existing on a level
just above the sewer.

Quite apart from the immediate effect of this scene, however, is
Kingsley's reiteration of this vision in different forms throughout
the novel and, more particularly, of his use of the sewer and putrefaction as a unifying device. In a later chapter, Jemmy Downes
returns to his dead family in their home, which is situated on
boards above an open sewer. In despair, Jemmy throws himself
into the sewer ditch behind the building, where he becomes indistinguishable from the offal and swollen carcasses of dogs floating
on a surface horridly illuminated by the phosphorescent glow of
rotting fish. From Jemmy's home typhus is carried to the homes of
the wealthy whose luxury is won at the expense of the lower classes.
Thus the link is made from these scenes and events to the nation at
large, and the social condition of England is symbolized by ad-
vancing decay and disease. Kingsley's employment of sensuously
perceived details to create an horrific vision and his use of putrefaction to symbolize the condition of England invests with power
the sociological evidence Kingsley had gathered from his various
sources.

Like Kingsley's three condition of England novels, his historical
fiction is fiction with a purpose. As such, it too teaches lessons and
points morals, but like the condition of England novels, his historical fiction derives its impact not from the substance of its message

but from its literary presentation. As a group, Kingsley's three historical novels form a pattern that illustrates the view that God is active in history. Each deals with a decisive moment in world history, and each reveals by comparison with Kingsley's age the issues and turmoil of the mid-nineteenth century. Each moment is both decisive and, like the nineteenth century's view of itself, transitional: *Hypatia* presents the fall of Roman Alexandria and the beginning of the Middle Ages; *Hereward the Wake* portrays the Norman Conquest and the emergence of post-Norman England; and *Westward Ho!* presents the vitality of the English Renaissance and, with the defeat of the Spanish Armada, the emergence of England's imperial power and her divinely sanctioned use of it on behalf of humanity.

Furthermore, in the historical novels, as in the condition of England novels, Kingsley used his powers of description to thematic and symbolic ends. In *Hypatia,* for example, the despairing Philammon helplessly watches the murder of Hypatia by a mob of monks before the altar of a church. Over the altar, a colossal statue of Christ watched

unmoved from off the wall, His right hand raised to give a blessing — or a curse? . . .
She shook herself free from her tormentors, and springing back, rose for one moment to her full height naked, snow-white against the dusky mass around — shame and indignation in those wide clear eyes, but not a stain of fear. With one hand she clasped her golden locks around her; the other long white arm was stretched upward toward the great Christ appealing — and who dare say, in vain? — from man to God. Her lips were opened to speak; but the words that should have come from them reached God's ear alone; for in an instant Peter struck her down, the dark mass closed over her again . . . . (X, p. 212)

This scene is thematically and symbolically significant. Here Hypatia, magnificent as the classical intelligence she represents, rises "snow-white" and golden-haired to be knocked down and brutally slain by the "dusky mass" that surrounds her and with which she contrasts in tone, taste, and temperament, as well as intelligence. But, placed in the novel at the moment when Hypatia is most receptive to Raphael's attempt to convert her to Christianity, this scene is even more pointed. In her distress, Hypatia lifts her arm to Christ as, simultaneously, the monks pull her down. Thus, Kingsley illustrates his belief that Christianity is superior to Neo-

Platonism because it has a message for the afflicted, and at the same time underscores his bitter critique of medieval Christianity by showing the monks destroying Hypatia at the moment of her conversion.

Kingsley paints most vividly, however, when his naturalist's imagination is engaged. *Westward Ho!* provides examples of Kingsley's talent both for using his powers of description to enliven the natural scene, powers employed most fully in his prose idylls, and for charging his description with thematic and symbolic effect in the context of a novel. In *Westward Ho!,* Kingsley's most evocative descriptions appear in those chapters that portray the tropical setting into which Amyas and his men sail:

> . . . all, sitting on the sandy turf, defiant of galliwasps and jackspaniards, and all the weapons of the insect host, partook of the equal banquet, while old blue land-crabs sat in their house-doors and brandished their fists in defiance at the invaders, and solemn cranes stood in the water on the shoals with heads on one side, and meditated how long it was since they had seen bipeds without feathers breaking the solitude of their isle. (VI, p. 23)

As if Amyas and his crew have landed in Eden before the Fall, the New World is unspoiled and full of wonders:

> Frank looked at the living gem, which hung, loud humming, over some fantastic bloom, and then dashed away, seemingly to call its mate, and whirred and danced with it round and round the flower-starred bushes, flashing fresh rainbows at every shifting of the lights. (VI, p. 24).

And so the crew lounges in Barbados for four days, eating strange fruit, observing unusual flora and fauna, and recuperating from their lengthy voyage. Recuperate they must, for Spanish Jesuits have brought the Inquisition to the New World and will, if permitted, enslave the natives and keep Eden for themselves.

Removed from the context of *Westward Ho!,* this scene could be expanded and turned into a prose idyll, its purpose changed to demonstrate the virtues of minute philosophy or, in more general terms, the beauty of God's creation. Located where it is in the novel, though, the description reinforces without direct statement the idea that emerging British power is, in challenging Spanish control of the New World, defending Eden from both Spanish domination and the consequent corruption of the Inquisition. This description therefore touches the central issues of the novel and ties what is otherwise an interesting interruption to the body of the story. Once again the impact of Kingsley's fiction derives primarily from the methods of its literary presentation.

As these scenes and others discussed elsewhere in this study indicate, an examination of the works of Charles Kingsley is valuable for the insights it provides into the mid-Victorian age, illuminating issues political, economic, social, and scientific. But it should also be clear that it is the impact provided by Kingsley's literary presentation of his ideas — their descriptive power as well as their structure — that has established him as an enduring Victorian writer.

Notes and References

Chapter One

1. Frances Kingsley, ed., *Charles Kingsley: His Letters and Memories of His Life* (London, 1877), I, [p. 37]. Hereafter cited as *Letters*.
2. Ibid., p. 21.
3. Robert Bernard Martin, *The Dust of Combat* (London, 1959), p. 28.
4. Kingsley, *Letters,* I, pp. 22–23.
5. Frances Kingsley, ed., *Charles Kingsley: His Letters and Memories of His Life* (London, 1908), p. 14. Hereafter cited as *Letters and Memories.*
6. Ibid.
7. Ibid., p. 17.
8. Ibid., p. 27.
9. Martin, p. 56.
10. Ibid.
11. Ibid., p. 60.
12. Kingsley, *Letters,* I, p. 122.
13. Martin, p. 61.
14. Kingsley, *Letters,* I. p. 123.
15. Ibid., pp. 123–24; Martin, 64.
16. Martin, p. 67.
17. Ibid., p. 65.
18. Kingsley, *Letters,* I, pp. 146–47.
19. Charles Kingsley, *The Life and Works of Charles Kingsley,* 19 vols. (London and New York, 1901–1903). All references to Kingsley's works are to this edition; volume and page are indicated parenthetically in the text.
20. Kingsley, *Letters,* I, p. 154.
21. Ibid.
22. Martin, pp. 78–82.
23. Kingsley, *Letters,* I, p. 155.
24. Ibid., pp. 156–57.
25. Ibid., p. 157.
26. Ibid., p. 162.
27. Ibid., pp. 184–95.
28. Martin, pp. 102–105.

29. Ibid., p. 106.
30. Kingsley, *Letters,* I. p. 197.
31. Ibid., pp. 206-15.
32. Ibid., pp. 215-19.
33. Ibid., pp. 221-22.
34. Martin, p. 112.
35. Kingsley, *Letters,* I, pp. 234-36.
36. Ibid., p. 234.
37. Ibid.
38. Martin, pp. 125-26.
39. Quoted by Martin, p. 126.
40. Ibid.
41. Ibid., p. 128.
42. Martin, pp. 129-30; Kingsley, *Letters,* I, pp. 288-91.
43. Kingsley, *Letters,* I, p. 292.
44. Martin, pp. 156-57; Kingsley, *Letters,* I, p. 338.
45. Kingsley, *Letters,* I, pp. 338-49.
46. Ibid., pp. 371-76.
47. Martin, pp. 169-70; Kingsley, *Letters,* I, pp.403-14.
48. Martin, pp. 171-72; Kingsley, *Letters,* I, p. 405.
49. Martin, p. 172.
50. Ibid., pp. 172-73; Kingsley, *Letters,* I, pp. 439-45.
51. Martin, pp. 191-92.
52. Ibid., pp. 201-202.
53. Kingsley, *Letters,* II, pp. 54-55.
54. Martin, pp. 216-17.
55. Ibid., p. 217.
56. Ibid., pp. 221-22.
57. Kingsley, *Letters,* II, p. 72.
58. Martin, pp. 225-27.
59. Kingsley, *Letters,* II, p. 137.
60. Ibid.
61. Ibid., p. 132.
62. Martin, p. 230.
63. Ibid., pp. 230-31.
64. Kingsley, *Letters,* II, pp. 179-80.
65. Ibid., p. 153.
66. Ibid., p. 191.
67. Martin, p. 237.
68. "Extract from a Review of Froude's History of England, vols. vii. and viii., in Macmillan's Magazine for January, 1864, signed 'C. K.' Pages 261, 217," *Newman's "Apologia Pro Vita Sua": The Two Versions of 1864 & 1865 Preceded by Newman's and Kingsley's Pamphlets,* ed. Wilfred Ward (London, 1931), p. 6. Hereafter cited as Ward.
69. "Dr. Newman to Messrs. Macmill and Co.," Ward, p. 7.

70. *"The* Rev. Charles Kingsley *to* Dr. Newman," Ward, p. 8.

71. "Dr. Newman *to the* Rev. Charles Kingsley," Ward, pp. 8–9.

72. "Dr. Newman *to the* Rev. Charles Kingsley," Ward, p. 15.

73. "Rev. Charles Kingsley *to* Dr. Newman," Ward, p. 16.

74. Ibid., p. 17.

75. "Letter of Explanation from Mr. Kingsley, as it stands in *Macmillan's Magazine* for February, 1864, p. 368," Ward, p. 19.

76. Martin, p. 244.

77. Kingsley, *Letters,* II, p. 191.

78. Ward, pp. xiii–xv.

79. Kingsley, *Letters,* II, pp. 270–72.

80. Martin, p. 252.

81. Ibid., pp. 257–58.

82. Ibid., p. 259.

83. Ibid., pp. 259–60.

84. Ibid., pp. 263–64.

85. Ibid., p. 264.

86. Ibid., pp. 265–68; Kingsley, *Letters,* II, pp. 265–67, 291.

87. Martin, pp. 267–69.

88. Ibid., pp. 270–74, 277.

89. Ibid., pp. 278–79.

90. Kingsley, *Letters,* II, pp. 421–41.

91. Ibid., pp. 441–61.

92. Ibid., pp. 449–60.

Chapter Two

1. Frances Kingsley, ed., *Charles Kingsley: His Letters and Memories of His Life* (London, 1877), I, p. 67. Hereafter cited as *Letters.*

2. Robert Bernard Martin, *The Dust of Combat* (London, 1959), p. 71.

3. Two illustrations are reproduced by Susan Chitty, *The Beast and the Monk* (London, 1975). One shows a naked St. Elizabeth, modeled on Fanny, carrying a cross up a mountainside, while being jeered by grotesque figures in the foreground: the other shows Elizabeth naked and crucified.

4. Kingsley, *Letters,* I, pp. 146–47.

5. Ibid., p. 147.

6. Margaret Farrand Thorp, *Charles Kingsley, 1819–1875* (Princeton, 1937; rpt. New York, 1969), p. 48.

7. Ibid., p. 42.

8. Ibid.

9. Cf. Guy Kendall, *Charles Kingsley and His Ideas* (London, 1947), p. 95.

Chapter Three

1. Unless otherwise noted, this section is indebted to Crane Brinton, "Chartism," *English Political Thought in the Nineteenth Century* (New York, 1962).

2. Mary Wheat Hanawalt, "Charles Kingsley and Science," *Studies in Philology,* 34 (1937), 607.

3. Patrick Brantlinger, "The Case Against Trade Unions in Early Victorian Fiction," *Victorian Studies,* 13 (1969), 45.

4. Ibid., pp. 45–46.

5. Richard Allen, Abstract to "Charles Kingsley and the Industrial Revolution," Diss. (Washington University, 1956).

6. Several discussions of Christian Socialism exist. A good, brief, and easily accessible one is Crane Brinton's; however, Charles William Stubbs, *Charles Kingsley and the Christian Social Movement* (New York, 1899) provides a fuller discussion.

7. On Kingsley's use of pastoral conventions in his fiction, see Gillian Beer's excellent "Charles Kingsley and the Literary Image of the Countryside," *Victorian Studies,* 8 (1965), 243–54.

8. Margaret Farrant Thorp, *Charles Kingsley, 1819–75* (Princeton, 1937; rpt. Octagon Books, 1969), p. 55.

9. Jack Harris, Abstract to "The Factory Hand in the English Novel, 1840–1855," Diss. (University of Texas, 1968).

10. Raymond Williams, *Culture and Society, 1780–1950* (New York, 1958), p. 100.

11. Frederick R. Karl, *An Age of Fiction: The Nineteenth Century British Novel* (New York, 1964), pp. 334–35.

12. W. Henry Brown, *Charles Kingsley: The Work and Influence of Parson Lot* (London, 1924), pp. 87–88.

13. Stanley Baldwin, *Charles Kingsley* (Ithaca, 1934), p. 110.

14. Hanawalt, p. 597.

15. Thorp, p. 129.

16. Baldwin, p. 120.

17. Una Pope-Hennessey, *Canon Charles Kingsley* (London, 1948), p. 152.

18. John O. Waller, "Charles Kingsley and the American Civil War," *Studies in Philology,* 60 (1963), 556–57.

Chapter Four

1. Unless otherwise indicated, I am indebted for this background material to J. B. Schneewind, *Backgrounds of English Victorian Literature* (New York, 1970), pp. 67–76.

2. Ibid., p. 68.

3. Ibid., p. 69.

4. Ibid., p. 71.

5. Ibid., p. 72.

6. Ibid., p. 73.

7. Mary Wheat Hanawalt, "Charles Kingsley and Science," *Studies in Philology*, 34 (1937); 600.

8. Frances Kingsley, ed., *Charles Kingsley: His Letters and Memories of His Life* (London, 1877), II, p. 156. Hereafter cited as *Letters*.

9. Ibid., p. 171.

10. Ibid., p. 174.

11. Ibid., p. 181.

12. A. J. Meadows, "Kingsley's Attitude to Science," *Theology*, 78 (January 1975), 21.

13. P. 594.

14. Kingsley, *Letters*, II, pp. 137–38.

15. Ibid., p. 174.

16. Ibid., p. 172.

17. Cf. Thomas Carlyle, *Past and Present* (London, 1843), pp. 205–206.

18. Cf. Kingsley's *Glaucus; or, The Wonders of the Shore,* a work of popular biology which sustains a tone and lesson similar to those of *The Water-Babies*.

19. Charles S. Blinderman, "Huxley and Kingsley," *Victorian Newsletter,* 20 (Fall 1961), 26.

20. Ibid., p. 25.

21. Arthur Johnston, *"The Water-Babies:* Kingsley's Debt to Darwin," *English,* 12 (1959), 216.

22. Ibid.

23. Ibid.

Chapter Five

1. I am indebted throughout this chapter to Allan John Hartley, whose paper at a Kingsley conference at the University of Leicester in 1975 set me thinking along these lines and whose *The Novels of Charles Kingsley: A Christian Social Interpretation* (Folkestone, England, 1977), is the best available explication of Maurice's influence on Kingsley.

2. Cf. Sheila Smith, "Blue Books and Victorian Novelists," *Review of English Studies,* 21 (1970), 23–40.

3. Frances Kingsley, ed., *Charles Kingsley: His Letters and Memories of His Life* (London, 1877), I, p. 264.

4. Una Pope-Hennessey, *Canon Charles Kingsley* (London, 1948), p. 120.

5. Margaret Farrand Thorp, *Charles Kingsley, 1819–1875* (Princeton, 1937; rpt. Octagon Books, 1969), p. 112.

6. Stanley Baldwin, *Charles Kingsley* (Ithaca, 1934), p. 127.

7. Joseph Ellis Baker, *The Novel and the Oxford Movement* (New York, 1932; rpt. 1965), p. 95.

8. Frances Kingsley, ed., *Charles Kingsley: His Letters and Memories of His Life* (London, 1908), p. 152.

9. Cf. Kingsley's portrait of George in *Alton Locke.*

10. Joseph McCabe, "Hypatia," *Critic,* 43 (September 1907), 268.

11. Ibid., and Baldwin, p. 138.

12. McCabe, pp. 268-70.

13. "Heroines of Nineteenth-Century Fiction: xx — Charles Kingsley's Hypatia," *Harper's Bazaar,* 34 (June 12, 1901), 80.

14. Kingsley, *Letters,* II, pp. 137-38.

15. Brenda Colloms, *Charles Kingsley* (New York, 1975), pp. 183-84.

16. Ibid., p. 183.

17. Quoted by Susan Chitty, *The Beast and the Monk* (London, 1975), p. 173.

18. Janet E. Courtney, *Freethinkers of the Nineteenth Century* (London, 1920; rpt. Freeport, N.Y., 1967), p. 25.

19. Walter Frewen Lord, "The Kingsley Novels," *Nineteenth Century,* 55 (1904), 998-99.

20. Lewis Melville, "The Centenary of Charles Kingsley," *Contemporary Review,* 115 (1919), 674.

21. Pope-Hennessey, p. 142.

22. Chitty, p. 170.

23. P. 156.

24. William J. Baker, "Charles Kingsley and the Crimean War: A Study of Chauvinism," *Southern Humanities Review,* 4 (1970), 252.

25. Baldwin, p. 155.

26. Ibid., p. 156.

27. Ibid., 155.

28. Melville, p. 674.

29. Baldwin, p. 157.

30. Owen Chadwick, "Kingsley's Chair," *Theology,* 78 (January 1975), 5.

31. Ibid.

32. Baldwin, p. 165.

33. Cf. *The Divided Self* (New York, 1969).

34. Baldwin, p. 167.

35. Ibid.

Chapter Six

1. Frances Kingsley, ed., *Charles Kingsley: His Letters and Memories of His Life* (London, 1877), I, p. 338.

2. Robert Bernard Martin, *The Dust of Combat* (London, 1959), p. 159.

3. Margaret Farrand Thorp, *Charles Kingsley, 1819-1875* (Princeton, 1937; rpt. Octagon Books, 1969), p. 140.

4. Frances Kingsley, ed., *Charles Kingsley: His Letters and Memories of His Life* (London, 1877), II, p. 55.

5. Ibid.

6. Ibid.

7. "Alexander Smith and Alexander Pope," *Miscellanies* (London, 1859), I, p. 287.

8. Ibid.

9. Ibid.

10. Ibid.

11. "Letter to Alexander Macmillan, Jan. 8, 1858," in C. L. Graves, *Life and Letters of Alexander Macmillan* (London, 1910), p. 116; quoted by Thorp, p. 139.

12. "Charles Kingsley's Place in Literature," *Forum,* 19 (1895), 564.

13. *Appreciations of Poetry* (New York, 1916; rpt. Freeport, N.Y., 1969), p. 294.

14. Martin, pp. 158–59.

15. Ibid., p. 158.

16. Kingsley, *Letters,* I, p. 339.

17. Ibid., II, p. 52.

18. Thorp, p. 141.

19. Una Pope-Hennessey, *Canon Charles Kingsley* (London, 1948), pp. 168–69.

20. Walter Houghton, *The Victorian Frame of Mind* (New Haven, 1957), p. 37.

21. Ibid., p. 35.

22. Cf. Herbert Sussman, *The Victorians and the Machine* (Cambridge, Mass., 1968).

Chapter Seven

1. David Anthony Downes, *The Temper of Victorian Belief* (New York, 1972), p. 51.

2. *Theology,* 78 (January 1975), 11.

3. Cf. Sheila M. Smith, "Blue Books and Victorian Novelists," *Review of English Studies,* 21 (1970), 23–40.

Selected Bibliography

PRIMARY SOURCES

1. Standard Edition

KINGSLEY, CHARLES. *The Works of Charles Kingsley.* 28 vols. London: Macmillan, 1880–1885. The most nearly complete edition of Kingsley's works; not the only acceptable text for his novels, however.

Other Acceptable Editions

KINGSLEY, CHARLES. *The Novels and Poems of Charles Kingsley,* with an introduction by Maurice Kingsley. 14 vols. New York: J. F. Taylor and Co., 1898. An acceptable text of the novels and more widely available to Americans than is the standard edition.

————. *The Life and Works of Charles Kingsley.* 19 vols. London and New York: Macmillan, 1901-1903. The edition used in this study; it presents an acceptable text and is more widely available to Americans than is the standard edition.

2. Letters

KINGSLEY, FRANCES, ed. *Charles Kingsley: His Letters and Memories of His Life.* 2 vols. London: Henry S. King, 1877. Standard source of printed material on Kingsley, this official biography lacks material included in later editions and abridgements.

————. *Charles Kingsley: His Letters and Memories of His Life.* London: Macmillan and Co., 1908. An abridgment containing useful information not in the official two-volume edition.

MARTIN, ROBERT B., ed. *American Notes: Letters from a Lecture Tour, 1874.* Princeton: Princeton University Press, 1958. Prints twenty-four letters, including unflattering remarks on America, previously withheld from publication.

————."Kingsley's Correspondence." *Times Literary Supplement,* 24 June 1949, p. 413.

3. Miscellaneous

KINGSLEY, CHARLES. *Miscellanies.* 2 vols. London: John W. Parker and Son, 1859. Contains some of Kingsley's critical articles and is a useful supplement to *The Life and Works.*

SANDIN, ERIC VERNER, ed. *Charles Kingsley's Only Short Story: An Abstract of a Thesis.* Urbana: University of Illinois, 1937. Prints short story text with an introduction.

WARD, WILFRED, ed. *Newman's "Apologia Pro Vita Sua": The Two Versions of 1864 and 1865 Preceded by Newman's and Kingsley's Pamphlets.* London: Oxford University Press, 1931.

SECONDARY SOURCES

1. Bibliographies
BARRY, JAMES D. "Elizabeth Cleghorn Gaskell, Charles Kingsley." *Victorian Fiction: A Guide to Research.* Ed. Lionel Stevenson. Cambridge: Harvard University Press, 1964. Standard survey of Kingsley scholarship.
————. "Charles Kingsley." *Victorian Fiction: A Second Guide to Research.* Ed. George H. Ford. New York: Modern Language Association, 1978. Brings up to date but does not supplant earlier *Guide.*
CAMPBELL, ROBERT A. "Charles Kingsley: A Bibliography of Secondary Studies, Part I." *Bulletin of Bibliography,* 33 (1976), 78–91; 104. Part II, 127–29. Includes list of contemporary reviews.
THORP, MARGARET FARRAND. "Bibliography of Charles Kingsley's Works." *Charles Kingsley, 1819–1875.* Princeton: Princeton University Press, 1937; rpt. New York: Octagon Books, 1969. Chronological listing of Kingsley's works, including information about contributions to literary periodicals.

2. Collections
BLISS, CAREY. "Acquisitions: February 16–May 15, 1953." *Huntington Library Quarterly,* 16 (1953), 437–40.
CLARK, ALEXANDER P. "The Manuscript Collections of the Princeton University Library." *Princeton University Library Chronicle,* 19 (1958), 159–60.
MARTIN, ROBERT B. "Manuscript Sermons of Charles Kingsley." *Princeton University Library Chronicle,* 23 (1962), 181.
PARRISH, MORRIS L., and BARBARA K. MANN. *Charles Kingsley and Thomas Hughes First Editions (with a Few Exceptions) in the Library at Dormy House, Pine Valley, New Jersey. Described with Notes.* London: Constable, 1936.
THORP, MARGARET FARRAND. "The Kingsley Collection." *Princeton University Library Chronicle,* 8 (1946), 18–20.

3. Biographies
CHITTY, SUSAN. *The Beast and the Monk: A Life of Charles Kingsley.* London: Hodder and Stoughton, 1975. Uses hitherto unpublished letters to explicate Kingsley's "private life," especially his frank appreciation of physical love and his practice of self-flagellation.
COLLOMS, BRENDA. *Charles Kingsley: the Lion of Eversley.* New York:

Barnes and Noble, 1975. Emphasizes Kingsley's attitudes toward the working classes.

MARTIN, ROBERT BERNARD. *The Dust of Combat: A Life of Charles Kingsley*. London: Faber and Faber, 1959. The best, most balanced biocritical study.

POPE-HENNESSEY, UNA. *Canon Charles Kingsley: A Biography*. London: Chatto and Windus, 1948. Emphasizes Kingsley's religious character.

THORP, MARGARET FARRAND. *Charles Kingsley, 1819–75*. Princeton: Princeton University Press, 1937; rpt. New York: Octagon Books, 1969. Sets out valuable, thorough discussion of publishing information and contemporary reviews of Kingsley's work.

4. Critical Studies

ALLEN, RICHARD EILERS. "Charles Kingsley and the Industrial Revolution." Diss., Washington University, 1956. Kingsley's protest against man's condition in a newly industrialized society as informed by the thought of Carlyle and Maurice.

ANNAN, NOEL. "Books in General." *New Statesman,* 27 (1944), 209. Kingsley's wits were inadequate to dispute with Newman.

BAKER, JOSEPH. *The Novel and the Oxford Movement:* New York: Russell and Russell, 1932; rpt. 1965. Kingsley's novels preach faith in the natural; Kingsley is Rousseauistic.

BAKER, WILLIAM J. "Charles Kingsley and the Crimean War: A Study of Chauvinism." *Southern Humanities Review,* 4 (1970), 247–56. Kingsley saw the Crimean War as a welcome challenge to England and wrote *Westward Ho!* to inspire "Tudor pluck" in his contemporaries.

BALDWIN, STANLEY. *Charles Kingsley*. Ithaca: Cornell University Press, 1934. Thorough study of Kingsley as a product of his age.

BANTON, MICHAEL. "Kingsley's Racial Philosophy." *Theology,* 78 (January 1975), 22–30. Kingsley's racial attitudes reflect the age in which the biblical account of Adam and Eve was coming under attack and in which scientists were attempting to explain the differentiation of the various races.

BEER, GILLIAN. "Charles Kingsley and the Literary Image of the Countryside." *Victorian Studies,* 8 (1965), 243–54. Kingsley's portraits of the rural poor counters the Romantic idea that the country dwellers' lot is one of dignity and harmony with nature.

BLINDERMAN, CHARLES S. "Huxley and Kingsley." *Victorian Newsletter,* 20 (Fall 1961), 25–28. Explores ideological differences between Huxley's agnostic rationalism and Kingsley's Christian transcendentalism.

BRANTLINGER, PATRICK. "Bluebooks, the Social Organism, and the Victorian Novel." *Criticism,* 14 (1972), 328–44. Study of the relationship between Parliament's accumulation of social data and novelists' use of it.

————. "The Case Against Trade Unions in Early Victorian Fiction." *Victorian Studies,* 13 (1969), 37–52. Early Victorian humanitarian writers sympathized with the working classes, but not with trade unions.

BRIGGS, ANN. "Charles Kingsley, the Muscular Christian." *Times Educational Supplement,* 17 June 1955, p. 650. Kingsley is memorable not for actions or writings but for the range of his activities and for the bold way he summed up the tendencies of his age.

BRINTON, CLARENCE CRANE. *English Political Thought in the Nineteenth Century.* London: Ernest Benn, 1933; rpt. New York: Harper and Brothers, 1962. Excellent chapter on Chartism explicates Kingsley's relationship to Carlyle and his *Alton Locke* as a Christian Socialist novel.

BROWN, W. HENRY. *Charles Kingsley: the Work and Influence of Parson Lot.* London: T. Fisher Unwin, Ltd., 1924. Kingsley's Christian Socialist activities.

BUCKLEY, JEROME HAMILTON. *The Victorian Temper: A Study in Literary Culture.* New York: Vintage Books, 1951. Indispensable background; the chapter "The Patterns of Conversion" is especially valuable for Kingsley studies.

CAMPBELL, ROBERT ALLAN. "Victorian Pegasus in Harness: A Study of Charles Kingsley's Debt to Thomas Carlyle and F. D. Maurice." Diss., University of Wisconsin, 1969. Carlyle supplied Kingsley with Natural Supernaturalism and the gospels of Duty and Work; Maurice gave him a coherent view of the word of God and clarified the meaning of the Church of England.

CAZAMIAN, LOUIS. "Kingsley et Thomas Cooper." *Nation,* 78 (June 10, 1904), 478. Thomas Cooper provided knowledge of London tailors trade for use in *Alton Locke.*

————. *Le Roman Social en Angleterre (1830–1850): Dickens, Disraeli, Mrs. Gaskell, Kingsley.* Paris, 1903. Trans. Martin Fido. *The Social Novel in England 1830–1850: Dickens, Disraeli, Mrs. Gaskell, Kingsley.* Boston: Routledge and Kegan Paul, 1973. Kingsley chapter of this important book concentrates on Christian Socialism, thus on *Yeast* and *Alton Locke.*

CHADWICK, OWEN. "Kingsley's Chair." *Theology,* 78 (January 1975), 2–8. As professor of history, Kingsley has been maligned.

CHAPMAN, RAYMOND. "Charles Kingsley and the Lavington Curse." *Notes and Queries,* 216 (1971), 91. Lavington curse is apparently derived from a curse on the Orme family, Lavington, Sussex.

COLEMAN, DOROTHY. "Rabelais and 'The Water Babies.'" *Modern Language Review,* 66 (1971), 511–21. In form and manners, Kingsley's story is indebted to Rabelais, one of his favorite authors.

COURTNEY, JANET E. *Freethinkers of the Nineteenth Century.* London: Chapman and Hall, 1920; rpt. Freeport, N.Y.: Books for Libraries

Press, 1967. Surveys Kingsley's literary production.

DESSAIN, C. STEPHEN. "The Newman-Kingsley Dispute." *Times Literary Supplement,* 24 February 1961, p. 121. Douglas Pett misinterprets Newman's *Apologia.*

DOWNES, DAVID ANTHONY. *The Temper of Victorian Belief: Religious Novels of Pater, Kingsley and Newman.* New York: Twayne, 1972. Study of Kingsley's novels in terms of theological position and use of the "plain prophetical style."

GILLESPIE, HAROLD R., JR. "George Eliot's Tertius Lydgate and Charles Kingsley's Tom Thurnall." *Notes and Queries,* 209 (June 1964), 226–27. Thurnall is the first physician hero in English fiction.

HANAWALT, MARY WHEAT. "Charles Kingsley and Science." *Studies in Philology,* 34 (1937), 589–611. Kingsley's scientific interests are important to character development in *Two Years Ago.*

HARRINGTON, HENRY R. "Charles Kingsley's Fallen Athlete," *Victorian Studies,* 21 (1977), 73–86. Kingsley's athleticism is checked by his admiration of "feminine virtue," a fact which returns the manly Christian back to a world of frustrating social existence and sexual anxiety. The return is a fortunate fall.

HARRIS, JACK THOMAS. "The Factory Hand in the English Novel, 1840–1855." Diss., University of Texas, 1968. Treats *Alton Locke* in a study of the characterization of the urban worker.

HARRISON, FREDERICK. "Charles Kingsley's Place in Literature." *Forum,* 19 (1895), 560–72. Although Kingsley was a writer of the second rank, he occasionally joined the first rank.

HARTLEY, ALLEN JOHN. *The Novels of Charles Kingsley: A Christian Social Interpretation.* Folkestone: The Hour-Glass Press, 1977. The best available study of Kingsley's novels as popularizations of the theology of Frederick Denison Maurice.

HEARN, LAFCADIO. *Appreciations of Poetry.* New York: Dodd, Mead, and Co., 1916; rpt. Freeport, N.Y.: Books for Libraries Press, 1969. Survey of Kingsley's poetry.

HEILMAN, ROBERT B. "Muscular Christianity." *Notes and Queries,* 185 (1943), 44–45. Use of the term by Kingsley, Disraeli, and Henry James.

HOUGHTON, WALTER. "The Issue Between Kingsley and Newman." *Theology Today,* 4 (April 1947), 80–101. Clash between Kingsley and Newman concerns more than the controversy of 1864; it is one aspect of the struggle between Protestant Liberalism and Christian Orthodoxy.

———. *The Victorian Frame of Mind, 1830–1870.* New Haven: Yale University Press, 1957. Invaluable study of themes and tendencies of the age.

HOWELLS, WILLIAM DEAN. "Heroines of Nineteenth-Century Fiction: xx. — Charles Kingsley's Hypatia." *Harper's Bazaar,* 34 (June 12, 1901),

79–83. Hypatia and Pelagia are two of Kingsley's most lifelike female characters; Hypatia is a sort of "Alexandrian Margaret Fuller."

JOHNSTON, ARTHUR. *"The Water Babies:* Kingsley's Debt to Darwin." *English,* 12 (1959), 215–19. *The Water-Babies* has survived as a book for children, but it grew out of problems at issue when written, particularly problems related to theories of evolution.

KARL, FREDERICK R. *An Age of Fiction: The Nineteenth Century British Novel.* New York: Farrar, Straus and Giroux, 1964. *Alton Locke* is remembered less for intrinsic worth than for exposure of contemporary conditions among working men.

KENDALL, GUY. *Charles Kingsley and His Ideas.* London: Hutchinson and Co., 1947. Kingsley as thinker on Christian Socialism, sanitation, Tractarianism, and eternal life.

LORD, WALTER FREWEN. "The Kingsley Novels." *The Nineteenth Century,* 55 (1904), 886–1004. Kingsley and all that he stands for explains much more than does the work of greater men.

MCCABE, JOSEPH. "Hypatia." *Critic,* 43 (September 1907), 267–72. Kingsley's Hypatia falls short of reality, thus becoming a device for revealing the impotence of Neo-Platonic religion.

MEADOWS. A. J. "Kingsley's Attitude to Science." *Theology,* 78 (January 1975), 15–22. Accepting the idea of a "struggle for survival" long before the Darwinian controversy raised the issue, Kingsley attempted to occupy a reconciling position between agnostic scientists and suspicious Christians.

MELVILLE, LEWIS. "The Centenary of Charles Kingsley." *Contemporary Review,* 115 (1919), 670–74. Emphasizes Kingsley's didacticism.

MIYOSHI, MASAO. *The Divided Self: A Perspective on the Literature of the Victorians.* New York: New York University Press, 1969. Study of literary manifestations of Victorian self-consciousness and of attempts by men of letters to define the self.

MORGAN, CHARLES. *The House of Macmillan.* New York: The Macmillan Co., 1944. Information about writers associated with the publishing house; includes letters.

PETT, DOUGLAS E. "The Newman-Kingsley Dispute Continues." *Times Literary Supplement,* 17 February 1961, p. xvi. In the pamphlet that was the immediate cause of the *Apologia* Kingsley changes his position from that printed in *Macmillan's Magazine;* this change is fundamental to understanding Kingsley's position.

———. "The Newman-Kingsley Dispute." *Times Literary Supplement,* 3 March 1961, p. 173. Newman lacks factual evidence to support assertions in dispute with Kingsley.

PEYROUTON, N. C. "Charles Dickens and the Christian Socialists: the Kingsley-Dickens Myth." *Dickensian,* 58 (1962), 96–109. Myth is that Dickens originated a school which Kingsley joined; the truth is that by inspiring Kingsley, he helped shape Christian Socialism and shared many ideas and ideals.

PRICE, J. B. "Charles Reade and Charles Kingsley." *Contemporary Review,* 183 (1953), 161–66. Kingsley exemplifies the "practical, social, and ethical bent" of recent English literature.

REBOUL, MARC. *Charles Kingsley, La Formation d'une personalité et son affirmation littéraire (1819–50).* Paris: Presses Universitaires de France, 1973. Study focuses on the formation of Kingsley's intellectual and emotional outlook and provides a thorough reading of *Yeast* and *Alton Locke.*

ROGERS, KATHERINE M. *The Troublesome Helpmate: A History of Misogyny in Literature.* Seattle: University of Washington Press, 1966. Portrait of Argemone Lavington in *Yeast* clarifies the belittlement underlying the "typical nineteenth-century exploitation of women."

SCHNEEWIND, J. B. *Backgrounds of English Victorian Literature.* New York: Random House, 1970. Excellent discussion of Victorian politics, religion, and morality.

SCOTT, P. G. "Kingsley as Novelist." *Theology,* 78 (January 1975), 8–15. Impact of Kingsley's social criticism lies in the manner of his presentation of experience.

———. "Tennyson and Charles Kingsley." *Tennyson Research Bulletin,* 2 (1974), 135–36. Tennyson and Kingsley's twenty-year acquaintance came through the friendship of both for F. D. Maurice and resulted in a few direct literary links.

SMITH, SHEILA M. "Blue Books and Victorian Novelists." *Review of English Studies,* 21 (1970) 23–40. Use of government Blue Book reports by Dickens, Kingsley, and Disraeli.

SUTHERLAND, J. A. *Victorian Novelists and Publishers.* London: The Athlone Press, 1976. Chapter 5 describes the effect on *Westward Ho!* of Kingsley's collaborative relationship with the Macmillans.

STEVENSON, LIONEL. "Darwin and the Novel." *Nineteenth-Century Fiction,* 15 (1960), 29–38. Impact of *Origin of Species* on Trollope, George Eliot, Kingsley, and Meredith as indication of the realization of social change.

STUBBS, CHARLES WILLIAMS. *Charles Kingsley and the Christian Social Movement.* New York: Herbert S. Stone and Co., 1899. Kingsley's involvement in the Christian Social Movement.

SUSSMAN, HERBERT. *Victorians and the Machine: The Literary Response to Technology.* Cambridge: Harvard University Press, 1968. Excellent study of the impact on Victorians of changes in intellectual and emotional life wrought by technological development; principal authors treated are Carlyle, Dickens, Ruskin, Morris, Butler, Wells, and Kipling.

TILLOTSON, KATHLEEN. *Novels of the Eighteen-Forties.* Oxford:

Clarendon Press, 1954; rpt. 1971. Incisive discussion of publication practices and background for "condition of England" novels.

UFFELMAN, LARRY K. "Kingsley, the Poet, and the Press." *Kansas Quarterly,* 7 (Fall 1975), 79–84. Attitudes toward popular and literary press in *Alton Locke* and *Two Years Ago.*

————, and P. G. SCOTT. "Kingsley's Serial Novels: *Yeast."* *Victorian Periodicals Newsletter,* 9 (1976), 111–19. Revisions of *Yeast* between publication in *Fraser's Magazine* and first publication as a book.

VANCE, NORMAN. "Kingsley's Christian Manliness." *Theology,* 78 (January 1975), 30–38. Center of Kingsley's ideal of Christian manliness is in Platonic doctrine of *thumos,* which Kingsley translated as "pluck" and asserted as the root of virtue.

VUILLIAMY, COLWYN. *Charles Kingsley and Christian Socialism.* London: The Fabian Society, 1914. Kingsley asserted the value of an aristocracy and believed in "restoring," not "reconstructing," society.

WALLER, JOHN O. "Charles Kingsley and the American Civil War." *Studies in Philology,* 60 (1963), 554–68. Kingsley was a Fremonter.

WILLIAMS, RAYMOND. *Culture and Society, 1780–1950.* New York: Columbia University Press, 1958. Chapter 5 studies *Alton Locke* as the conversion of a radical, materialist Chartist engaged in class warfare and strikes to a Chartist along Kingsleyan lines.

WILLIAMS, STANLEY. *"Yeast:* A Victorian Heresy." *North American Review,* 212 (November 1920), 697–704. Kingsley's religious debates are less concerned with theological dogma than with attempting to relieve the plight of the poor by applying the principles of Christianity to the purposes of industry and trade.

WOLFF, ROBERT LEE. *Gains and Losses: Novels of Faith and Doubt in Victorian England.* London: John Murray, 1977. Sets Kingsley's fiction, particularly *Hypatia,* within the broader context of Victorian religious ferment.

Index

58, 60, 62–64, 91, 93, 95, 102–103,
110–11, 113, 115, 118–21
Wordsworth, William: "Michael,"
54–55

Wright, Thomas: *Family of Hereward,
The,* 113

Yonge, Charlotte, 57